THIS STUFF IS REAL, MY TESTIMONY

THIS STUFF IS REAL, MY TESTIMONY

NANCY C RAY

This Jesus Stuff is Real,

My Testimony: How Jesus Rescued Me.
Written by: Nancy C. Ray

Introduction

The bible tells me and other Christians that we overcome our fleshly motivated and evil behaviors by allowing God to transform us into Jesus's image. This transformation process is our testimony to the goodness and majesty of God in a life. God receives all the glory for the work of his spirit.

Our, all Christians, testimony is unique to our individuality. God comes into our lives where we are. He knows all about us. So, this book is a response to him asking me to share my testimony of how He, God, has worked and manifested himself to me. This task, to share my testimony with others, is my volunteer assignment in my life. All my words have been inspired by the Holy Spirit to convey to the reader what God has revealed of himself to me.

I want the reader to understand the hopelessness of my condition. I hope they feel this to understand the transitions that I experienced. I hope they will be able to rejoice with me in the learning of my triumphs along the way.

Foreword

God was asking me to write a book for him. In it I was to reveal all I had learned in the Holy Ghost school of life. I was reluctant at first to accept such an undertaking. While reading a friend's book, I found myself hearing my thoughts within me, these thoughts were speaking inside my head. They were thinking, "I would have said it different in my book." I had used the words my in my sentence. That meant, I was considering accepting the call from God to write this book.

Then, I dreamed about a great banquet table in a great dining hall. My host was at one end of the table, and I was at the other end. He was asking me a simple question. "Nancy, what are you doing with your life these days?" My response was quick, clear, and precise. I responded, "I am reading chapters from my book on my podcast." Shock of my life. I awoke from the dream and had my answers. I was being asked to write a book that I had no desire to write. I knew nothing about this task. But over time, God would send different people into my life to guide and encourage me to follow this path. My worship leader in TN told me one time, that I should write a book. My Pastor here in KY also told me the same thing. So, it has been confirmed by two witnesses that this is God's calling for me.

It has been established that God desires for me to write my testimony of how my encounter with Jesus has changed my life. God will receive all the glory and praise for His works in my life. The first thing I must remember is my past. Trying to recover my memories is extremely difficult for me.

All these writings are the result of the real truths that God has taught me over the lifespan of forty years. They were helpful and insightful to explaining who God is and his motives and plans for mankind. I acknowledge that God's wisdom and knowledge is needed for me to be able to write one word of this story. I am totally dependent upon Jesus to provide me with the words of life that will be needed to convey meaning to my testimony story.

Before Jesus

The purpose of telling the past is to be able to demonstrate the contrast with the present life and how it is conducted now in the present. The before and after had to be examined carefully. How dark was my darkness? I needed to know and be aware of my past and the life I had previously led. I had to remember and dredge up some horrible memories that I had tried to forget. Now my soul was searching through those memories to glean the important spiritual growth opportunities that I experienced.

By not choosing God, I was experiencing darkness in life. A lost person does not understand these terms, so just think darkness and depression are similar. I needed to able to discern the changes of darkness to light. I needed to be able to appreciate the transformations. So, I needed to be aware of the selfish sinful way of life I was living before Jesus became my savior. What was my life like before the cross? To examine these truths, I must go back to my life's foundations that I was pursuing.

My Religious Upbringing and Background

I was raised privileged and with good morals. I was a member of the country club and played tennis and swam in the pool. I was educated and groomed to become the wife of someone who could become famous like a mayor or senator. My parents had high expectations of me.

I was forced to attend church as a child, but it never took. I thought, if I loved God and wanted to serve him; I would have to become a nun. In my understanding, women who loved God served him in this capacity. Well, that was definitely not my idea of fun, so I threw it all out of my thinking, my religious upbringing, societies' morals, the proper way of behaving, it all went out the window. Everything that I was taught about religion, I rejected. When it came to mandatory services in high school every Friday morning, I became a champion at sleeping through the entire service. Ignoring all content being dosed into me; I spit it all out. I had been through confirmation classes earlier in my childhood, and those were gone also. I had attended many VBS classes in the summers, and sang in children's church choirs, all of it was dismissed. I was definitely not a believer.

So, you can see there was no spiritual foundation, spiritual anchor, to protect my soul. I was a free soul out in a strange vast land of dry arid places without a clue to the horrible evil spirits that were pursuing me to destroy my soul. I was without God or his Son. That makes me a lost person destined for a life of misery and despair. I was empty inside and filled with violence, hate and revenge. I was not a forgiving person to others or to myself.

So, the scriptures state the unbeliever is perishing, I was definitely in that category. I was setting myself up for falls, continual heart aches, and misery. I was destined for Hell, and I knew it. There was a popular rock and roll song that fit me perfectly. It was, "I'm on the Highway to Hell." I remember singing it as I was driving down the road.

I vaguely was aware of the Ten Commandments, and I knew I had broken every one of them sometime or other in my totally rotten, God forsaken life. But I wasn't going to say I believed in something that I really did not believe in at all. Jesus's resurrection was definitely not in my beliefs.

I was defiant, I was of the women's liberation generation. I was taught by society that we, the women, were in charge of our bodies; free love was beautiful, and we did not have to be hindered by moral codes. Whose rules, were they? They were just ignorant people who needed a crutch called religion. Society told me I was smarter than that. I believed the lies of society. I was a graduate of college, and I knew what the system had told me. Nobody educated would believe that book called the Bible. The messages from society were loud and clear. It is your life; you make your own decisions.

So, I played hard and fast. I was driven by rock and roll, sex, cigarettes, drugs, and alcohol. You would find me with a drink and a cigarette in my hand. My mouth was disgusting. I had a cussing habit that was vile. Every word out of my mouth was a lie. I could make up one so fast to protect my ugly nature from being discovered, just like that.

When you are young and dumb you think you can do anything and get away with anything. We are so wrong. Now that I am writing this book, I remember all these horrible behaviors I was exhibiting.

I don't even know how I made it home some days. I should have been dead many times. Driving under the influence was as dangerous as they say it is. I was ruining my health gradually. I was no longer fit. You see

I was introduced to alcohol early in life. I thought the more grown up you are, the better you can handle your whiskey. Unfortunately for me, I liked mine mixed with coke. I never realized it was the soda that made me thirsty, and I would quickly drink my drink and still want more. If I had just known, drink just a coke and enjoy yourself as you are, you will be so much happier. All my life, events were foggy in my memory due to the alcohol.

By the age of college, I was already a full-blown alcoholic. It had started with beer in high school, and had gradually moved on to wine, rum, whisky, bourbon, and tequila. It seemed no activity could be performed without alcohol being included in the festivities. If you asked me if I had a good time, my answer would depend upon how drunk and disorderly I got. I was thinking that was what we called partying or having a good time. All social events revolved around alcohol.

Alcohol played such an important role in my development. Or should I say how it hindered me and caused me much pain and suffering. I want to convey how I was a slave to the drink, and it owned me, not the other way around. I was not in control of my alcohol consumption.

There was a spirit involved in my drinking. It, being Satan, used me and lied to me about his whereabouts. I did not even know he was around until after I was saved, and God opened my eyes to reveal to me my true enemy of my soul. God taught me that my enemy only wanted to steal, kill, and destroy my life. He was not for me in any kind of way. He was the enemy, and he used alcohol to control me and keep me his prisoner. He was the Father of Lies and deception. He was excellent at playing his part in my life. He could be all over the place, and yet I was unable to detect his presence. He was wreaking havoc upon my life from the back lines. He was always having the last laugh when I was defeated and stabbed me in the back over and over again. I thought it was fate. I thought I was doomed to bad luck. I thought the gods were mad at me for not paying them any attention. Little did I know, it was truly Satan himself and all his little demon helpers that were ruining my life through alcohol.

Why can I blame alcohol for all my troubles because it is the common factor in all my experiences and milestones of life. It was responsible for my attitude and behaviors. It determined my viewpoints on different subjects in life. It caused me to miss out on all the times in life when we achieve special milestones in life. They are made into special occasions, and your family members rejoice with you for your accomplishments. But alcohol stole those times from me. It accompanied me in all my experiences. It is amazing that I even made it to twenty-eight years. I was dangerous on the road to others and myself. But I never would have admitted that truth to anyone. I was in denial. I lied, comforted, and excused myself. I told myself it was all part of life, and everyone lived this way. We were all doing it, living this way, and it was perfectly normal.

No, it was not. Did I care about other people at all? No, if they got in my way of having a good time then they were disposable. My cruelty toward others was horrific. I was rebellious of everything that stood for the good in life. My job was to break the rules and think only of myself and my pleasures. I was mean, cruel, and full of hate for my fellow human beings. Where did all this hate and resentment come from? It was flowing out of my heart. I had gradually developed a heart of stone.

I was not interested in pleasing anyone. I did as I pleased with no regard for my decisions affecting other people. But the world kept patting me on the back and telling me what a wonderful job I was doing in life. They would reinforce my lifestyle in the different forms of media. I would see myself as an indifferent actress playing different roles in her life. I would hear it in the music and the lyrics of the songs that played on the radio. Television shows were full of women living like me. All the messages coming into my soul were saying and claiming that I was living the good life, and I was better than so many other people. It was all lies, and I could not see them. I could not discern the evilness of these messages. I had no filters in my life anymore. Self-control was going quickly in many different areas of life.

Relationships were far, few, and in between. I had a few drinking friends. I had several men, but no great love. I would not have even known what love was. I was too busy being self-absorbed in my little world.

Years progressed, and they were all a blur. Life was moving quickly, and it was passing me by. I had a few different jobs, I was married, pregnant, had a child, divorced the next year. That was all in three years. I had stopped drinking during the pregnancy because I was aware of fetal alcohol syndrome in babies. Although I did not stop smoking during this time, the drinking stopped completely. I guess you might say, I began waking up sober and saw the world differently. But as soon as the baby was born, I returned to the drinking harder than ever, consuming stronger and more potent drinks. I was definitely an unfit mother. I had no business trying to take care of a baby. But it was required, and so I found many babysitters to take my place in the rearing of children.

Once again alcohol was ruining my life. I was trapped in its webs of deceit. More years passed in a blur. There are just a few memories of those times. But most of the time, it is clouded by the drink. It stole from me the precious forming years of my daughter. It gave me no joy within my soul. I was an empty shell of a person, and I felt like I was dead inside.

I was a dancer from the age of three. I loved dancing, and my body loved to move to the music. It was just natural. So, when I discovered bars with bands and everyone could dance, I thought I was in heaven. Every weekend I was somewhere dancing, drinking, smoking, and partying till the bars closed in the wee morning hours. I was defeating myself by allowing myself to get too drunk. I was hot and thirsty after dancing vivaciously on the dance floor. So, I would need a beer to down to quench my thirst. I was a real sot. We would order pitchers of beers each night. I would consume them like it was a competition to see who could drink the most. I thought this was how all people acted. I was out of control. I was too wild.

One night, we were driving home, and I was pulled over by the cops. Before I knew what was happening, I was being taken in for driving while intoxicated. I spent the night in jail to cool down, and then my father had to come and bail me out. I was a big disappointment to my parents. The courts found me guilty of DUI and took my license. I was able to obtain a restricted license that allowed me to travel to work and school during the work week, but I was illegal to drive on weekends.

My insurance premiums doubled, and it was a real hassle trying to get places. But it did not stop me or cause me to stop drinking. I was hooked. So, I just went to my boyfriend's house and stayed with him all weekend, and then I came home that Monday. He did all the driving, and we continued to drink and party with our friends.

I did not know anything about reaping what you sow. This is another Christian phrase meaning Karma, I was oblivious to all spiritual concepts. I was blinded and continued head on, living my life of rebellion.

I call it rebellion, because I knew society said not to act the way I was behaving. The right thing to do was behave and drink responsibly and not to excess. In my mind that was not fun. So, I refused to obey the rules of society and made my own rules and decisions. I was the master of my life, not someone else. Spiritually, I was putting myself on the throne and declaring I was God of myself. This is the mistake so many people make in their lifetime.

Rebellion is refusing to obey. I was rebellious in most of the moral sanctions that were there to guide my life. I could not help it. What I was rebelling against was God and his commands. Something evil in me was driving me to behave this way. I was out of control, and I could not have stopped myself if I had wanted to stop or change directions. This is the power of sin. Sin dwells in our bodies. We are determined to do the wrong thing. Something inside of us causes this behavior to manifest. It is wicked, and in the end, it hurts the person deeply.

One of the worst influences on my drinking was agreeing to become a debutante to please my mother. All the girls who were being presented to society that year would throw a party every weekend for the entire year. Most of them revolved around alcohol and partying. This only contributed to my drinking problem. It was an open bar and free booze every weekend. My fiancé and I consumed way too much. If you were to ask me about any memories of the parties, I would have to admit, I do not have any. I was too drunk to remember.

My father died when I was twenty-two. He had been a prisoner of war in WWII. He told us that while being in captivity, he had prayed to God that if he would rescue him from his prison, that he would raise three children. They would all be dedicated to serve him. I remember when he uttered those words, and I made some sly sinister response about how wrong that had all gone. Yes, he had three children but none of us were serving God at the time.

Losing my father at such a young age had an impact upon my life. His words were like knives. His prophecy about my upcoming wedding and the disaster that he foresaw were cruel. I did not receive his blessings. And then he was dead, and those words could not be taken back. He was fifty-four and dead from a heart attack. I later learned of the sufferings he endured as a prisoner and came to realize the environmental factors had greatly contributed to his health issues. Being half an orphan had another type of impact upon me.

We buried him and drank away the pain and sorrow. I had three months to prepare for my upcoming wedding. Mother and I remained busy and pushed through.

My wedding was a complete blur. Just think, the most wonderful day of your life and you missed it. We were married in early 1979 just after college. I walked the aisle of a fancy church and had a reception that was fit for a princess, and I am a total blank to the people that attended.

I went to work for a bank as a teller. I learned fast and was able to perform my job accurately and professionally. I was what they called a functional alcoholic.

Our marriage was a disaster. All we had done was party together. We had no foundation built between us. When the fights began, they were vicious and cruel. The man you have given your life to has now become your worst enemy. Meanwhile, I have now brought another human being into the world. We spent his paycheck by the end of the weekend and lived on mine the rest of the week. It was daycare and babysitters because I did not know how to be a good mother. As soon as the baby was born, I returned to my drinking and wild ways of life.

Alcohol would continue to plague me until I was twenty-eight years old. It was a merciless master. It stole from me my youth, and it gave me back heartaches and miserableness my entire young adulthood. It was my master because it owned me. I did not own it. It allowed me to be free while I was pregnant with my first child, but after the birth, it returned harder and stronger than before. It owned my soul, and it was not going to ever let go of me. It consumed my life just like the cigarettes were doing.

Spiritual Encounters

Over the years, different dreams came to me. The first one, was when I was in my early twenties, Jesus came to me and said, "Who do you say that I am?" I answered that he looked like Jesus, but I was not going to say that I believed in him if I truly did not. I told him, "I don't know." So that is where he put me. He put me in the I don't know room and left.

Then years later, he came again and asked again. I answered you are supposed to be Jesus, but I cannot say I believe in something, if I do not truly believe in it. If I did believe it, this belief would make me act different in my behaviors and words. I knew if I genuinely believed, I would not act like I did. It would be important to me. This much I knew deep inside my heart.

But I was lost, another term meaning without God in my life, and did not know what to do in different situations. We called our marriage quits and the divorce was finalized. I became a single, divorced mother with a one-year-old. What a disaster I have made of my life, I thought. I am not a success. I have been rejected by my partner. I have been betrayed and abandoned. I will have to carry on some way. In my viewpoint, life was horrible, and I was to blame for most of it. I had not tried hard enough. I had just let it all happen to me, like it was out of my hands. It was fate that was dealing me a deck of cards that anyone would have trouble playing. I was miserable inside. My thoughts were negative and self-destructive to my self-esteem. This was the beginning of the reaping from the bad seeds sown.

I got a new job and moved to Florida. Over the years, I rented various places and abused the babysitters while I continued to frequent bars looking for love in all the wrong places. I was miserable and alone. I had made friends, and then I had lost them because of my moving for work purposes. I finally ended up in Columbus, Georgia, and there I finally met the God, I had so longed for in the deepest part of my heart, that had hardened to stone all those years ago.

My Testimony

It was at the age of twenty-eight, Jesus revealed himself to me in such a profound way that I had no choice anymore. I could not deny him any longer. It took a few months to culminate into my final surrender. Here is how it proceeded.

I was visiting a friend's house for a wedding. I came back to her house drunk, as usual. She had been attending a new church and had gotten saved earlier that year. Saved means she asked Jesus to be her God. She was telling me about her church, and what she was learning. I understood some of what she was saying, but mostly I just saw her glowing like an angel. It was really weird. I just thought it was the effects of the alcohol, and I dismissed it at the time.

Then another day, I was reading an article in a magazine, and it was talking about the power of forgiveness. I did not know much on the subject, so I followed along and practiced forgiving all the people in my life who I had a grudge against. I had to be honest and deal with all the ugly truths. I got through the article and forgave my offenders. I said their names out loud and meant it in my heart.

A little later, maybe a year, I am back at home in Georgia. My lungs hurt from smoking, so I just call out to the Universe and tell him my lungs hurt, as I breathe out. By this time, I had developed a chain-smoking habit, and I was consuming two and half packs a day. I bought cartons instead of packs. Later that night, I heard this voice speaking to me on the inside. He said, "don't smoke." I said OK, but I think that will be hard for me. I got up the next morning and did not smoke. I put my cigarettes in my purse and went off to work. About three o'clock that afternoon, I decided I really needed a cig, but he, the voice, said, "don't smoke." So, I went into the bathroom and asked for his help. I just prayed a simple prayer telling him he said not to smoke, but I really wanted to, so could he please help me. Bingo, the urge to smoke was removed from my person. It was quick and powerful. I was thrilled. I was delivered from smoking just like that. I went to the bars to check out this new deliverance. It worked, I did not smoke the entire night, day, and the next day. It was a miracle, and I knew it. I decided this inner voice was God speaking to me.

I had enough knowledge to know that God was at church. My friend had said I needed a full gospel church to teach me the truths. On my way to bowling league, I had to pass this small country church with a sign that read full gospel. So, I took myself to The Open Gate Full Gospel Church in Columbus, Georgia to thank God for this wonderful powerful deliverance from nicotine. I knew that quitting smoking was extremely difficult, and many a person suffered terribly with withdrawals and cravings. They had told me how the nicotine withdrawal would turn my fingernails yellow. Others had said that addiction to cigarettes was as strong as someone trying to quit cocaine. For me, I was great. My nails were clean, and I was free from all desires to consume a cigarette. I was so thankful that I had no symptoms.

When the preacher asked if anyone wanted to say a few words about how good God was, I stood up and told the congregation about my deliverance, and that I had come to thank him for this miracle. I sang with them and listened to the sermon.

I decided to return and investigate more. After a few more services, I was confronted with this Jesus issue again and again. The songs were being sung about him. I just wanted to worship the Father. I was thanking him for the cessation of smoking. He was who I loved. So, you see, I still was not saved at this time.

Then in another service a very unusual thing happened. I did not realize how spiritually powerful this event was at the time, but since then, I have come to understand that not everyone has this powerful revelation given to them. It was miraculous and way over the realm of the natural world.

I am singing with the congregation, and we are just having an enjoyable time, but all of it is about worshipping Jesus. Well, I just cannot get over this hump. So, while I am singing, Jesus himself, the same voice inside of me that I heard in those previous dreams, is talking to me. The man leading the worship is speaking in tongues, and I hear Jesus talking out of him. He is explaining to me the resurrection. He says, "You believe that God has all power?" So, if God wanted to raise Jesus from the dead, did he have the power to do so? I answered inside my head, "Yes, God has all the power, he is God." So, he says, well, "The Father raised me from the grave." It was like a lightbulb came on. My mind, brain, spirit, and soul all now understood his message. The Father raised the son from the grave. That is why Jesus is alive now. God the Father raised Jesus, the son, from the dead, and whoever believes this truth receives the gift of God which is eternal life. So, I said. "I believe that." Then I heard a voice come into the back of my head at the base of my neck, and he said, "Good, I am here now."

Wow my eyes were opened! I understood that Jesus was alive. I was a believer. What a rejoicing feeling inside of me was taking place. Even though I did not tell anyone that day what happened, I just left the church, like I was walking on clouds. The world was gorgeous, nature was so clear and clean. God's world was changed by my new perspective. That was when I was twenty- eight years old.

Now I was delivered from smoking and had also met Jesus. I had believed for the first time in my life that he was alive. I did not know much at that time. I had forgotten all my teachings from Sunday school. But

I remembered the Apostles Creed because we said it every Sunday my entire life. The words were now coming to me differently. I believe in God Almighty maker of heaven and earth. And in Jesus Christ his only son....

I made a vow to God. I told him if he ever saw me with a cigarette in my hand again, then it meant that I no longer walked with Jesus, my Lord. I was determined to never return to smoking again. I was so thrilled to be delivered from that nasty habit. I would have nightmares where I had smoked in my dreams. I would awaken worried I had broken my vow. Gradually, over time, the dreams faded. I was free forever from the addiction. I never craved one cigarette or wished to smoke again. My God had set me free.

Now what? I have a lot of repenting of my sins to confess in prayer. I had to confess all kinds of horrible sins out loud to God. I knew that I would be forgiven if I would come clean to him. I remembered the Ten Commandments, so I started with them. Every infraction I could think of, I confessed and said I was sorry. Many a tear was shed, as I realized what a horrible human being I had become in my short existence here on His planet. It was extremely painful to have to bring up those deep hidden memories.

I said to myself I need a manual to teach me how to think and behave. I do not know anything about this spiritual place and the rules that govern it. I need help. I was told that the Bible would explain to me my salvation experience and teach me everything I needed to know about Jesus and this new life I was experiencing. I had so much deep joy inside it was remarkable. I was no longer miserable.

The bible said that I deserved death for violating God's law. I knew I was wicked and deserved punishment. You see sin is like a cancerous seed planted in our inner being. When left alone, it will begin to mutate and attack our lives in many different forms. It is not a good seed, and it does not bring forth good fruit. It is vile and corrupt and will cause us trouble in our lives. My seeds were many, and they were raising their ugly heads no matter how much I tried to stomp them back down.

I knew that Jesus was alive, there were no doubts there ever again. I knew I was extremely guilty of breaking his commands. My attitude towards other people was terrible. I was uncaring, I was using people to get what I wanted. I was not a good person. Sure, I had a few friends over the years, but most of my life, I was guilty and ashamed of my horrible conduct. God taught me about the motive for my actions is what made it a sin. He showed me all actions had to be motivated by love. This was his measuring stick.

I came to God in prayer day after day as different memories began to reveal themselves. What was so amazing was that I did not find condemnation. I found mercy. God listened and probed for my motives for the behaviors. He explained that they were a heart issue problem, and he was able to mend the broken hearted. Wow! Mercy and compassion were extended to me. He was taking my sins, nailing them to the cross, and giving me his righteousness. I did not deserve any of it. He said it was because I believed that the Father had raised the son that these things were possible. Amazing Grace was offered to me. He forgave me for all my transgressions.

It was an exciting time in my life. I confessed more and more. I saw how wicked I was inside. I realized that the flesh had taken control of my life. I had bought into the lies of the world. I had kicked God out of my life and his rules and regulations. Now I was asking him back in to stay forever. He was cleaning me from the inside out. My mind was being reprogrammed to think like one of his spiritual children. I was communicating with God in prayer constantly. I was reading his words in the bible, learning more and more about Jesus, and what it meant to follow him.

He took my sins and nailed them to the cross. He took the punishment for my sins, the death that I deserved, and he placed them on the cross. He died in my place. I had helped to kill my Jesus; every sin in the future, present, and past was on that cross. Jesus dealt with all the sins of the world. That is why he died. He died for every human being that would be birthed for all time. They only had to believe, and they too, would benefit from Jesus's ultimate sacrifice.

This newfound freedom that I was experiencing internally was causing more joy to manifest on the outside. I was beyond myself. I was clean and forgiven, and this just made me love Jesus more and more. It was like God had plowed up all my bad cancerous seeds of sins, and the garden was now fresh and ready to receive the good seeds. My heart was clean. I was clean. There was hope in the world again.

Alcohol

The first thing that went was the alcohol. The hard stuff was gone immediately and with no withdrawals. I continued attending church and listening to the preacher and Sunday School teacher. I was learning about this new way of living. I was a big sponge soaking up as much as I could handle. I had true joy inside of me. I was at peace with God.

It was wonderful, but sometimes I would notice that I would change and get mean sometimes from deep inside of me. When I spoke to God in prayer about the situation, he gently showed me that I was still drinking alcohol, just a lighter version in the wines. He said, "Why do you think the Indians called it spirits?" Oh dear, I thought, the wine is allowing the evil spirits that had my life prior to get a foothold in my life again. I need to get rid of all alcohol forever. The alcohol was actually stealing my joy in the Holy Spirit. I didn't want to jeopardize that wonderful feeling. Obviously, I cannot handle any alcohol now in my life. I obeyed, and I made another vow to God to remain clean of that wicked poison of my soul.

Since I made that decision, I have had the blessing of understanding others who deal with this monster on their back. It is an addiction, and it is cruel and wicked. Most sufferers do not even know they have the problem. They are blinded by the enemy and kept in the darkness of understanding. Under the influence of this drug, many a person has acted, said ugly comments, and hurt other people's feelings. They have made enemies of their loved ones. They have suffered terribly due to the lies that it has projected to the consumer. When you get in their way and try to help them, they respond negatively and attack mentally the one who is assisting.

That demon called alcohol, who has set up his throne in this person will protect his territory of that human being's life that he rules over. He has no intentions of leaving or vacating the premises. He has come to stay and reign, and that will be where he will remain, until something stronger than him comes along and dethrones him. That someone is Jesus. He can throw the demon off the throne and return the human back to a sane mind. It's just a matter of them asking him to do this act of kindness. The truth that I learned is alcohol is mean, and it does not care about you at all. You are Satan's slave, and he is your master.

Now there is also another side of alcohol that must be addressed. You see alcohol consumption is only one of the effects of a much bigger issue. It is the heart not wishing to bend its will to God. It is the rebellious nature that lives inside of us all. We want to be God, and we want to decide which rules are right and wrong. We will have the final say so in our life, and if it breaks one of God's rules or principles, then we just dismiss his existence and rule our own souls without him.

Now most people who have not chosen God to be their God will argue this point. That is not what I am doing, they will protest. I am not trying to play God they will argue. That is ridiculous they would banter. You don't know what you are talking about they would accuse the person who loves them and is trying to help them stop their behaviors. You are making all of these grand statements about my behaviors, and you have not got a clue what my problems and difficulties are in life. They probably want to curse me at this point.

The drinkers make excuses over and over again. The lost person will defend his right to decide what is right and wrong. The rebellion demonstrated is strong and adamant.

While a person remains influenced by alcohol, they are extremely vulnerable to making very wrong decisions and bringing harm to themselves and others. It is a vicious cycle that takes hold of the person. They think they are in control, but actually the alcohol is a tool of Satan that he uses to manipulate and control his victims. He wants them to be rebellious and defiant.

God wants them submissive and honoring Him. Satan wants God not to be honored, revered, worshipped, or praised. God wants his creation free from the whips, prisons, chains that Satan inflicts upon his creation. His will is to deliver a person to himself, so they are free to know and love him eternally. God has only good intentions for his believers.

Baptism of Holy Spirit

During these initial learnings by the spirit, I was introduced to the baptism of the Holy Spirit. Since I was attending a Charismatic church where speaking in tongues was encouraged, I also wanted this gift from God, just like I had heard in my salvation message. Now at the time, I had no idea what a controversial subject this was. I was not aware of all the warnings different churches were issuing. I had found and heard Jesus by a man speaking in tongues. I had understood his message to me as clear as if he was speaking English. I was about three months old in the Lord.

I never knew the hostilities that would occur, because I was endorsing this event. Even today, certain publishers that I would love to be interested in my book will not touch it, because of this chapter. When I share this part of my life, some people are scared of me and think I have a spirit. My own husband, who was a good Baptist, thought I had a demon until it happened to him. He got up in front of the entire church and apologized for his negative expressed thoughts against the spirit of God. During the late 1970's there was a revival in the land, and many Christians experienced the baptism of the spirit.

For me, I heard about this book called, *Nine O'clock in the Morning* that was explaining this transformative experience, so I went to the local Christian bookstore and purchased a copy. I read it with great zeal and practiced the prayers and sought understanding. It did not happen immediately. I had to genuinely seek for it. I prayed and asked God to fill me with his spirit. You see you have to allow the spirit to control your tongue. Well, I was hesitant. So, while praying, I asked God to allow me to receive this precious gift that I would need to overcome the evil powers working against me. I said I do not know the words to say. Then that same small voice said, "Can you read it?" I said I would try, and a ticker tape ran in my mind, and he said, "read that." Then the power of the spirit was upon me. I read the lines in tongues. Wow, the words came so fast. I was speaking in tongues. I was thanking God for this great gift. I could speak to God in a spiritual language, and it was precious. I could praise him in this divine language. I talked all night long. When I arose that morning, I was still speaking in tongues. It was there, and it was not something I did. The spirit in me was speaking to the spirit in God, and the communication was perfect.

Then when I attended church, and we would have high worship, I could sing to God in tongues also. It was the most beautiful language, and it allowed me to open my heart wide to God. It was a direct link spirit to spirit without any hinderances. I was alive in the spirit, and it ran throughout my body quickening me. I was free of sin and death. I was free from the judgment of God. I was tasting that the Lord was good. More scriptures were being fulfilled every day as I worshipped God.

The anointings were strong and powerful. People attending were experiencing the move of the spirit. It was like a revival every service. I was growing deeper in God, and my eyes of understanding were being opened. It just made me love the Lord more. This love for Jesus made me want to follow him even more. And the more I followed, the more I wanted to obey his words of instruction.

My God was wonderful, and I would gladly lay my life down for him. He was unbelievable. Our fellowship and communication were so powerful. He would reveal more of himself to me. The scriptures were alive to me. When Jesus would speak to his disciples and ask them if they would leave him too; they answered where would we go, you have the words of life. I too answered this and many more questions bowing and honoring Jesus for who he is.

Consecration

Confessing my sins and agreeing to serve and obey the Lord's teaching was how my prayers continued. I learned there are three categories of sin motives. They are the lusts of the flesh, lust of the eye, and pride of life. These sins keep us from fully experiencing all that Jesus has for us.

I would find this process of confessing and yielding my life to the Lordship of Jesus was called consecration. I was dedicating myself to him and allowing him to clean me and call me holy in his eyes. Allowing God to cleanse me and give me his holiness through the righteousness of Jesus caused me much rejoicing. He was making me aware of my new position.

God was with me all the time. Sometimes in the services, I could literally feel his presence during the worship service. We, my fellow believers, would refer to this feeling as a rain shower. God's spirit would show up at the services. It was like a drug for me. I wanted more and more. I searched out different churches and attended many services. Some places had more showers than others. I would categorize them as raindrops, mistings, or full rain. Later, I would learn these perceptions were called the anointing. Jesus was the Anointed One, and so it makes sense when his presence is perceived in a service, that it would be called the anointing.

Meanwhile, it felt like the Lord was wanting me to give all of my life to him. He wanted it all and for me to become his. I said yes, because I had done such a terrible job of it, that I knew I would be much better off letting him run it instead of me. So, I made him my Lord and my master. Jesus was all mine. I had made a deal with him. He was my God, and he was a living God. That meant someone was actually hearing my prayers and receiving my worship. We had a living relationship. This is the faith that he seeks from us. He wants us believing in Jesus.

I was haunted in my dreams, and I would wake up thinking I had sinned. It was my first spiritual battle. In my dreams, the enemy would attack me in many different forms. I would be scared for my life. I would end up telling them about Jesus, before I would stop fighting them. I always survived. I had men with chain saws chasing me in between the rocks and boulders. I would tell them about Jesus, and they were gone. I was learning how to overcome the enemy by calling on Jesus. Sometimes in my dreams, I would go flying and soaring in the heavens with Jesus. I loved these times. It seems like he was always teaching me some scripture, and the spiritual life truth it revealed.

Family's reaction

Naturally, I wanted to share what had happened to me with my family members. I thought they would be pleased and happy for me. Their reaction was very shocking and disturbing for me to hear. My mother, who was an outstanding church goer, who had sung in the choir all her life, responded to my born-again experience with these words, "I thought I educated you better." She was very disappointed that I had fallen to believing in Jesus. I was very surprised and later realized my mother was just lost like I had been. She couldn't understand spiritual matters, because she had not allowed the spirit of God to introduce himself to her. I was determined to make this a daily prayer request to God. Please save my mother was my prayer.

Later in the years she accused me of constantly telling her what a sinner she was. I knew the Holy Spirit was working on her. Finally, months before dying of cancer she let her pride down and prayed for God to save her. It gave me such comfort at her funeral that she had preplanned before her death she had the words repeated, No one comes to the Father except through the Son. It gave me such peace to know my mother had made Heaven too.

My brother was a little more tolerant, and he thought I was just a bit confused. It was his opinion that I had been saved when I was baptized as a baby. He again said that during Confirmation classes I had rededicated my life to Jesus. I assured him that I had never accepted Jesus until now.

Later on, in his retirement years, he began attending a Bible study. He became very spiritually aware and quoted different verses. I knew then he had experienced the new birth, and he was walking with Jesus. When he died at the age of 69, I took great comfort in knowing beyond a shadow of doubt that he too made Heaven his home. It was a great comfort for me to see my family make Jesus their Lord.

My sister was hostile at one point. She said she and mother did not like the person I had become. I just had to respond with the scripture that I would give up family to follow Jesus and I chose him always. She finally asked Jesus to be her savior. I rejoiced with her. She was reluctant to ask Jesus to be her Lord and gradually let it all return to how it was before. When she consumed her wine, her true nature was revealed, and the hostilities toward me increased. They could definitely see that I was different. I was bold in the spirit and showed a lot of zeal for God. I think they were a little bit scared of me.

Friends disassociated themselves from me. I knew they would; I had been warned. Other so-called friends who claimed they were Christians just tolerated me. They thought I needed to calm down. It was nothing to get that excited about. I thought to myself these people asked God into their lives when they were just children. They have lived with him always. They don't understand the transformation I am experiencing. Their testimony is different from mine. God had come in like a steam roller, and they had just peacefully acquired Jesus into their lives.

I would learn later that some of this complacency they were showing was because they never read the scriptures and were never ignited with the spirit of God. For a lot of them, I questioned their salvation. To me, so many people who went to church were still dead in their sins and not living for God. It was a sad situation. Again, I was determined not to become apathetic about Jesus and his loving message.

Worship Experience

One day, at the worship service, I was in God's presence and just quietly as always, he asked me a question. When the Holy Spirit is asking questions, he is trying to teach you the answers based on what scriptures you have been reading and contemplating. Me, I had been thinking about how Jesus was the door. I was in my spiritual mind approaching the cross of forgiveness and judgment of sins. I was kneeling, and he called me closer. I stepped up to the cross and entered through the cross to find myself in the kingdom of God.

I was different, the place was different, I was in the realm of Jesus's kingdom, and I was aware of the transformation that was taking place. I had approached the cross, and I had gone through the cross to the spiritual realm. I was clothed in the robe of righteousness. I was able to see and understand the environment and the rules of this new entity's realm. I was in God's realm, and here, God was king. He ruled here, and I was a visitor.

This was his kingdom, and I would be consumed by fire if any sin was found in me. Just me entering into his perfect kingdom would mar its perfection. I approached cautiously and reverently. I walked in faith towards his promises that I could come into his presence. I was on the highway of holiness on my way to see the Father.

I approached his throne and applied the blood of Jesus as my covering, and I continued moving forward to my God. I worshipped him up close. I was no longer far away worshipping from afar. I was in his realm; I was at his throne; I was alive, because he willed it. I was refreshed and ignited. I was humbled and forgiven. I was cleansed and welcomed into his presence. I was filled with his life-giving spirit. This was a place I never wanted to leave. This was the ultimate peace, love, and joy experienced by being in my God's presence. My heart was broken. I rejoiced and cried at the same time. God was revealing himself to me.

I could look behind me and see how I had entered into this glorious place. I had come through the cross. I had come because Jesus had made the way for me to come. He had given me his covering; he was the door to the kingdom. I had entered through that door. From now on, I would know how to enter God's throne room. I was so thankful and enlightened by the scripture that Jesus had quoted that he was the door and that no man came to the Father except through him. Scriptures were being lived out in my life. This was just reinforcing my faith I had in Jesus, and the reality of his existence in my life. This experience made more scriptures come alive.

During one of these worship services, we spoke of the hot coals from the altar being placed on the lips of the worshipper. It was from the book of Isaiah. I asked God to cleanse my lips with his coals too. I believe there was a great spiritual transformation that occurred from that prayer. My mind and tongue were being cleansed, and I was careful how I spoke to others. I did not want to offend anyone with my tongue. My words to God were also cleansed and spiritual worship became stronger and more reverent in my approaching his throne. My words could speak life and death now. His scriptures again were quickening inside of me. He had said life and death were in the tongue. We spoke from the fountain of living water inside of us.

Hymns of the faith also became alive. I remember the hymn; *I Have Decided to Follow Jesus*. It also referred to the cross being before him and the world behind him. Now the cross was behind me, and the throne of God was before me. Truly Jesus was the door. So many scriptures became alive in me. The word of God was being demonstrated as I worshipped. My God had allowed me to view his place.

Over my lifetime, I have only had a few revelations so strong as this one was. It was truly a unique spiritual experience. It meant a great deal to me, and I will always cherish it deeply in my heart.

Worshipping

Since then, I have come to learn so much more about true worship. God says that he is seeking true worshippers. They need to worship in spirit and truth. So, it became very important to learn how to give my love to God uninhibited. First, I learned it was not about me. I was to center in on him. He was the target. Second, I needed to think about how I was going to worship him, when I got to heaven. There was an old hymn about, *When We all Get to Heaven,* and they talk about how they are going to sing, shout and praise. So, I decided I was not going to wait till I got to heaven to give him my best. I should do it here too, while I'm here on earth. So, if I wanted to dance in front of God, I did. If I needed to shout his praises, I did.

I found that clapping is a great way of showing your appreciation, so why not clap for the king. Welcome Him to your service, clap for his arrival, be genuine not fake, and do not make up something that is not happening. Be real. God likes honesty. Rejoice about God. Concentrate on something you have been studying and give him the glory for that event. Let your mind worship also.

There are certain words that Christians use when experiencing God's anointing. We will say, "He is Lord". And sometimes in the highest realm of worship, we will use the highest word of worship which is Hallelujah. This word is extremely strong. Only the pure in heart can use it correctly and speak it by the power of the spirit. Only a person who is truly committed to Jesus can call him Lord and mean it. God takes these words very seriously. He is listening to our praises and worship. He knows our hearts and motives. He knows when we are genuinely worshipping, and when we are just going through the motions.

Worship allows us communication with God. It is our way to come together with other believers, and together we come into agreement about Jesus, God, and the Holy Spirit. This unity is a corporate agreement which pleases God immensely. Remember, he said where two or more are gathered in my name he was there with them. God is in our services. We need to remember this every time we start our meetings. We need to be in good standing with God before we attempt to enter into his kingdom realm. We need to be clothed with his righteousness before we can enter into his realm. He calls this process wearing the robe of righteousness. We need to show reverence toward God. We need to be grateful and thankful towards God and his salvation gift he has bestowed upon his believers.

Giving

Another way we worship God is by giving of our time, money, emotions, and our lives. Now the money part is the hardest part. We all work hard for our money, and we never have enough. We need money to buy all the necessities of life. We use our money to determine the value of objects. We will spend more money on something that has more perceived value. Now the desire for things can become lopsided. If we spend all our time acquiring things and possessions those things, those items can begin to have power over us.

For example, pretend you bought a new sofa. You spent a lot of money on that sofa. Now your kids come in and jump on the sofa and break the springs. Your reaction will demonstrate how you feel toward your things. Do you lose your temper and scream at the kids? Do you walk away and sulk about your sofa and how you can never have nice things? Do you wish you had protected your sofa better? Do you punish your children for breaking the furniture? How much power do these things have over us?

When we realize that things are more important to us than people, then we learn an important lesson. Our desires are strong for material goods. We need to stop them from taking over our lives. We should own the stuff, but not let the stuff own us.

When we look deep inside of ourselves, we can see some spiritual powers at work in our members. Covetous is the desire for stuff that others have, and you want for yourself. Some people will break the law to acquire things. They will actually steal it from the company or the person who owns it. This unchecked desire will lead us down the wrong path in life.

Now the bible says the love of money is the root of all evil. That is a very powerful truth. It is ok to have money to meet your needs, but the love of money will bring evil behaviors in your life. So, God has devised a plan to conquer this evilness called, the love of money. He claims that this love of money is the little 'g' god, called Mammon. By giving to God's kingdom, we give Mammon or Satan a black eye. They are a god of greed. We acknowledge that God, the creator, is our God, not Satan, devil or other names he uses. We put our finances under God's control. He then has the authority to bless us in the financial realm. This includes all sources of incomes, from our jobs, investments, and everything that the devil could possibly be in control of is now in God's hands. Because we gave our finances to him, and we put him in charge of our finances.

We defeat the god of covetous and greed by giving to God, the living God, and he will decide what is done with it after that. We take our hands off. We look for good ground to sow into. This could be your local church or other ministries. The workers who are doing the job of spreading Gods' words to others is always a good place to sow your money. We allow God to bring the different harvests; he wants to reap. We do not tell him anything. We remain submissive to his authority over our lives.

Where you are receiving your spiritual food is a good place to invest your money. If there is a certain preacher you have been following and growing with in the spirit, then by all means support his ministry. He is doing God's work and should be compensated. Now that makes us a cheerful giver. Knowing that God owns it all, and he only allows us to manage some of his property. It is easy then to give where it is needed.

Salvation Blessing

Salvation experience is just the beginning of your walk with God. Without it you could not go anywhere spiritually. But because we believed, and we have stayed believing, we are able to experience all the good things that God wants to give us. He loves us so much. We are his people, the sheep of his pasture. He is the shepherd; we are the sheep. He will provide for all our needs.

He will protect us in the spiritual realm. Satan has no power or authority in God's realm. Stay with Jesus, and you will not encounter the enemy. Walk away and the demonic forces will eat you for lunch. They hate God, and they hate his children. You as a believer are inheriting everything from God. They are getting nothing but the dry arid places. They are stuck here on the earth. They only can mess with humans who are disobeying God. A believer is free from these evil forces. This is just one of the many promises that God has made to his children.

The bible has promised believers many blessings. They can all be found in the book of Deuteronomy and Revelation. God makes a grand gesture about the blessings he wants to give his people. To the obedient and faithful they will receive the eternal life. Eternal life cancels out death. It is the only thing that can overcome death. This precious gift of Jesus cost him his fleshly life and existence here on this earth. Thank the Father he took Jesus back to Heaven to reign with him forever.

Overcomers according to Revelation will receive different special gifts. One such gift is the ability to eat from the tree of life which is in the midst of the Paradise of God. Another promise is that the believer will not be hurt by the second death. They will receive the hidden manna to eat and a white stone with a new name written . He is also given the power over the nations and the morning star.

They shall be clothed in white garments, there name will remain in the Book of Life and Jesus himself will confess our name before the celestial deities. More promises to the overcomer are to become a pillar in the temple, his new name and be granted permission to sit with Jesus on his throne. In my opinion, those are promises worth obedience. No other religion does this.

Most religions are composed of a man seeking to have an audience with their so-called god. In Christianity, it is the true and living God seeking humanity to have a living relationship with them for eternity. This God has made a way for his people to be able to fellowship and enjoys his presence.

Forgiveness

One of the first things I experienced from God was forgiveness. He said that I was forgiven, when I confessed the sin and repented of doing the wrong behavior. God said that the sin hurt me and others. He said that sin grieves God's heart, and he does not like to be around anyone who is guilty of sin. So unconfessed sin blocks our communication with God. But as soon as we acknowledge our guilt, and tell God we are sorry, our communication is restored completely, and it is like it never happened. This process is called justification. You are treated as if you never have ever sinned before by God.

When we believed on Jesus and received his righteousness in exchange for our sins, we also were justified. You see Jesus took the judgment for your sin. It has already been taken care of, and it would be an insult to God to not receive his forgiveness that he longingly loves to give to his children. It is completely free. Jesus paid for it.

That is great. I am forgiven for my sins I acknowledge. Now he asks me to forgive others as he has forgiven me. What? I cannot do that, I balk. Do you know what that person did to me? He hurt me badly! I was betrayed, abandoned and other horrible things, and you want me to forgive him? I question God's commands. That is too much God. It was not my fault. He attacked me, I reason. How can I forgive him?

It is not possible. I am not capable of doing this, I argue. You are asking too much from me, I think. I know the scripture is really clear about how I am required to forgive, so my Father in Heaven can forgive me, I reason. What a mess I have gotten myself into now. Will I obey?

Help me Jesus to be able to do this? I inquire. So, Jesus speaks to me and asks me a question. He says, "Do I, Jesus, forgive him for these sins?" I answer yes sir; you forgive everybody who asks. He said, "Do I live inside of you?" Yes, you live in me. Your Spirit, that gives me life, dwells inside of me. He answers, yes, that is true. I need for you to let the Spirit of God dwelling in you forgive this man. Oh, I just forgive with your Spirit and agree with you on this forgiveness issue. I see now. I will let the Christ in me forgive the human man of his detestable sins. Yes sir, I can do that.

So, I prayed a simple prayer and forgave the ignorant man for committing sins against me and Jesus. It worked. I, myself, also forgave him. Now that is the power of forgiveness. I let him go out of my life, but he left forgiven. He was no longer my burden to carry. I had given him over to the Lord, and he would deal with him now. You see if we play God and do not offer forgiveness because we are judging them and sentencing them to prison, then we block God from operating in their life. We are not God. We do not get to withhold forgiveness from anyone.

The Triune of Man

During this first year of encountering Jesus, I learned some of the very basic truths of the spiritual realm. My first big lesson was learning about myself and what made me tick. You see, we are made up of three parts, the flesh, the soul, and the spirit. The way he explained it to me was through the smoking deliverance example. He said my flesh, the human part that runs my life all the time has these cravings and desires. In smoking it desires a cigarette. It sends a message to the brain about its desire. The brain processes the request and tells the body yes or no. Now before Jesus, the brain was in complete agreement with the flesh, and it would give and do anything the flesh requested. These are the sins we act out.

Now the brain is located in the soul. The soul is the mind, the will, and the emotions. So, the emotions enjoy smoking and the social satisfaction it brings. So, the emotions are in agreement with the mind that the flesh should smoke.

Now the third part of the soul is the will. This is where the choices are made. What do you want? If that is what you want, then that is what you will do. Therefore, the flesh will run the show, because the mind, will, and emotions agree with the flesh's choice.

But when you asked Jesus into your life and made him Lord of your life, you were given his spirit inside of you. Now this spirit is from God, and it desires to please God. It knows what God wants. So, when you were born again, your spirit was ignited. The spirit now plays a role in your decision making. My spirit is filled with God's spirit. I now want to do what pleases the Father.

So, the flesh sends the signal, I want this. The mind receives the message. But this time the will says, no we do not want the cigarette. We made God our Lord, and he does not want it, and neither do we. Then the spirit chimes in and says don't smoke. So, we now have his spirit and the soul, two thirds of our being telling the flesh no. The deciding vote is the will. If the will says no also, then they shut the flesh down, and tell it, the flesh, it cannot have what it desires all the time. The flesh is no longer running the show; the spirit is in charge, and the mind has decided to obey the spirit and will. Now you have the majority of your triune being going for God's side.

The flesh does not have a chance. It will not get its way anymore. Oh, the flesh will try repeatedly to get its way, but if the believer lets the spirit lead, then the believer will not obey the lusts of the flesh anymore. So, the entire decision is made in the will. When we say let God's will be done on earth as it is in Heaven, we are spiritually battling the lusts of the flesh.

Now in the natural world of Psychology our Father of that science, Freud, proposed his own triune of man also. He called it the id, ego, and super ego. The id was the flesh running rampantly wild indulging in all the pleasures it could acquire. The ego and super ego tried to keep the id in check. But you see that is the natural man. That does not consider the spiritual realm and His power over the situation. So, psychology ignores the spiritual realm of mankind. God laughs at mankind for thinking they can figure out man. God created man, and he knows what makes a person behave the way they do. He has the truth, not behavioral sciences.

This overcoming of the flesh is just another benefit of salvation. When Christians claim they are free, it is also they are free of the choices the flesh will make, that will cause the person to engage in a sinful behavior. Before Jesus, we were at the mercy of the flesh. Now we are free by the spirit of God to overcome temptation. That is a lot of freedom. No longer a slave to the flesh. Set free from the chains of sin. Delivered just like that, from all of the evil influences in our lives. So, we shout freedom in our services. We mean we understand how free believers have become. We are thanking our God for this power he has given us to overcome. That is the scripture paraphrased, he whom the spirit sets free is free indeed.

Triune of Sin

Christians who read and study their bibles are believers who learn there are three motives to sin. These are Lust of the flesh, Lust of the eye, and pride of life. (I John 2:5-17). I found out that these are the three reasons for my flesh to act and desire its sinful cravings.

Let us examine a specific sin. For example, let us take lying. Why do we lie? Because we want something, because we want to be someone, and have pride and power in life. Maybe we are trying to hide or deceive another. Or maybe we see something and want it enough to lie to get it. All these thoughts and reasons will lead to sin when the body acts on these desires.

Take another sin. How about stealing? We see it, we covet it, and we take it for ourselves instead of paying for it. These are our lusts, our wants, and our desires. We have many, and we take them for granted. We act upon them every day. It is our choices that we make, that will decide if it becomes a sin in God's eyes.

God's Viewpoint

God made this world. This is his earth. He wants the inhabitants of this planet to love Him and others. It is that simple. We are not loving to Him or others when we break spiritual laws. These laws are put into effect by the angels, and it is their job to monitor the spiritual dimension. That is their job. The fallen angels love to accuse the humans of breaking a spiritual rule. The way the earth is set up, if you break a rule then the punishment is death. The wages of sin is death the Bible declares. That is the law that operates upon this earth. God set it up, the angels enforce it, and the judgment occurs when violated. That means no matter how good a human tries to be, they will never be able to obey all the rules and commandments of God. It is impossible, because we are not God. We are all condemned to die at the judgment because we have broken God's rules.

This world is run by another little 'g' god. His name is Satan, Lucifer, or the Devil. He is the one who has taken humans captive to their sinful lusts. He is the one running things and keeping us prisoners to continue in sin and reap the judgments. He hates humans, and he wants to see their destruction.

I did not realize it back in that first year of my new life. I was changing Gods. I was choosing the Father and getting rid of the Devil. Now the Devil did not want to let me go. I had been doing a great job serving him and shunning God. I had embraced all of his lies, I had been ignorant of his schemes, and I was doomed to the judgment.

Now along comes Jesus, and he gets my attention. I am choosing to go with God in my life. I am getting rid of the evil powers that seek my life. I am choosing to live God's way. I am rejecting Satan and his powers in my life. I am believing the truths that God's word is proclaiming. Jesus had said the truth will set you free. I was gradually becoming freer in the spirit and empowered by the word of God to go forth and overcome the flesh, and the wicked thoughts and powers that were warring for my soul.

Yes, it was a war. I was being torn apart. Everything I had learned all my life had to be refiltered. The bible says to take every thought captive to the word of God. I had a lot of thoughts that needed refreshing and cleansing. The wars with my mind were many. It always boiled down to the final building block of Jesus. The crucial question was Jesus alive or not? The answer that I responded would make all the difference in all my thoughts, attitudes, and behaviors I would exhibit. Thank God I knew, beyond the shadow of a doubt, that he was very much alive, and that was good enough for me to keep going.

The Armor of God

Over time I learned about the armor of God. I learned all the pieces, and then I learned how to pray and put them on every day. One day, while telling God about the pieces and their purposes, I realized that I did not have to keep putting them on. I could live in them and thank God for each piece. I would then tell him why these objects were so important to my spiritual walk and what they meant to me personally. I made the armor mine. I claimed the promises of the armor and examined each piece carefully.

Take for instance the helmet of salvation. This piece gives me knowledge of God's word, transformation of my thinking process, and the ability to take all thoughts captive to the word of God. God's word was the measuring stick. It had the final say about all subjects. It determined everything.

Here is an example of how my mind would fight me all the time. I would claim that Jesus was alive, and the hateful brain would respond. Then if he really is truly alive, then why don't you believe him and do all these mission works? You are a hypocrite. You are not a Christian. Why would God want you? You are not good enough. No one could believe you. You belong in a mental hospital. On and on the lies and accusations would come. I was so confused and ignorant of the scriptures to understand how to handle these thoughts.

So, I fought with what I knew to be true. I would take the worst fears and extend them to their worst scenario, and then I would answer, I will still tell everyone about Jesus, no matter where they put me. Later on, I would come to understand these negative thoughts were called doubts and disbeliefs. They were to plague me for the rest of my life.

So, to church I would go. In worship service, I learned that I must worship God in spirit and in truth. I realized that meant for me to worship God the way he called himself. I would take a characteristic of God and concentrate on that attribute during the service teaching myself what the word of God said about this trait of God. Then I would worship him around that teaching. Songs would become alive, and truths would come forth in the songs. Hymns had so much more power than before. I was worshipping my Jesus and consecrating my life and love to him. I remember one such service, I was telling him how much I loved him, and he answered in that same familiar voice. I had begun to recognize his voice, and he said, "Oh you love me, well that will have to be proven." Prove my love for God. What does that mean? "Yes, Lord, I love you," I responded in song and worship. He responded, "prove it."

Jesus had asked Peter if he loved him. He asked three times. Each time Peter declared his love to the Lord. God's response was always feed my sheep. That was what God wanted from me too. He wanted me to feed his flock. He wanted me to study scriptures with others, teach others his truths, encourage them in their faith, and help wherever possible. That would be the way to show my love to my Lord.

Would the living God ever trust a human being to not deny him or fall away from their love for Him? He knows the human heart, and he knows how dark, conniving, and evil we truly are. He knows that all men are liars. He says we are deceitful and cannot be trusted. His scriptures throughout all the books describe a human as wicked and corrupt. There is no good in them. They are sinners. Now I am telling him I love him with all my heart, strength, and power. It is a commandment, and I am claiming I can obey this command. Can I really love the Lord my God? We will see over your lifetime how much you really love the Lord.

I did not realize at the time, but God had entered me into the Holy Ghost school of hard knocks. I was a stubborn person who needed to be convinced of all the truths that he was trying to teach me. So, my life became a series of lessons to learn by experiences. Now I had to be reading the scriptures to be learning, enveloping, and experiencing these truths.

Kingdom of God

For example, take the scripture about seeking first the kingdom of God. During worship service, I would think about what is the kingdom of God? John the Baptist had preached it was coming. He said the kingdom was near. When Jesus arrived, he declared that the kingdom was now here on the earth. So, when the King walked on the earth he was over his kingdom. So, I started thinking about an earthly kingdom.

When there is a king, the territory that he reigns over is called his kingdom realm. This is where his authority, power and rules dominate the area of rule. This area or his realm is called the kingdom. So, what area does Jesus rule over? He rules over the spiritual realm. That is why it is so hard for a human to understand, let alone believe, because the kingdom of God, they cannot see this in the natural. It is a spiritual concept that must be revealed by the Holy Spirit. He will not reveal any of this to you, if you are not a believer in Jesus's resurrection, and that he is alive today up in Heaven ruling over everything in the Universe. That is how big his kingdom is. Remember he created it all, so naturally he rules over it all. There is nothing happening that he does not know about.

Now if two kings were debating with one another about who was the greatest king; they would declare their kingdom size determines their might. Then what about the people who live in the kingdom. How do they fare? Are they happy and enjoying the benefits of the king's glory or are they miserable servants who must do the bidding of the king or die. Are the people free to choose their king? Or is he the master who does not care about the lowly subjects in his realm. What makes a better king? Think about it.

Then later in my reading of the Bible, I came across another scripture that sent me deeper into the spiritual truths God had laid out for me to learn. It stated that the kingdom of God was righteousness, peace, and joy in the Holy Ghost. Well, I was already experiencing joy during the worship services. My heart was full of joy when I was walking with Jesus. I had great peace when I surrendered to God in different matters of life. But this righteousness, I did not know what that meant, or how powerful it truly was in all believers' lives.

I studied and found that righteousness means you are in good standing with God. You are perfect and without sin in God's view. Jesus was righteous, and he gave his righteousness to me. That means the Jesus never sinned his entire life. His blood was innocent, and he should not have been killed. He was innocent because his Father was God, and his mother was a virgin innocent also at the time. The blood line passes through the male paternal father. This leads me to the second piece of armor. It is called the shield of righteousness. It is a defensive weapon to stop the enemies' arrows from piercing my heart. It can deflect them or quench the fires. The believer needs to be aware of this spiritual truth in their lives.

How did we receive this righteousness from Jesus? Jesus was perfect and never sinned. That is why, when Satan killed Jesus, he violated a spiritual law. You cannot kill an innocent man.

Satan was in charge of the world. He made sure all sinners were killed and taken to the grave. Jesus allowed Satan, in fact he tricked him, into killing him. Now Satan is guilty of law breaking.

This new knowledge has only come to me in the last few years. Yes, I now believe that Jesus wanted Satan's followers to kill him. One of the scriptures says if they had known they never would have crucified him in the first place. I pondered on this thought for a long time. The evil forces knew who Jesus was. They had been warned by God in the Psalms to kiss the Son less he becomes angry, and you are destroyed in your way. God had commanded complete obedience to Jesus on this earth. God had spoken aloud during Jesus's baptism, and He had proclaimed him as His son. His last words were a warning listen to him of heed him. Who do you think God was talking to? The people thought it thundered. They did not hear God. The spiritual world heard the words, and they knew they referred to the Psalms.

Then you read a few parables of Jesus about the vineyard and it belonging to the Father. The son comes to rule the vineyard and they decide to kill the heir and get rid of the rulership and take the vineyard for themselves. When you study this parable a little closer you can see that God's vineyard is the earth. The rulership is up for grabs. He makes suggestions to the powers of the world how they can acquire and get rid of the new ruler. Jesus actually is planting the idea into their heads to kill the son and take the ownership. They are not thinking straight. Jesus had planted a seed in the evil spirits domain and now they are determined to carry out this plan. They will kill Jesus, the son of God, and take away all the rule of God, and they will have the whole world and the earth under their dominion. They will throw off the yoke of God and be free of his limitations, they think. They are making a big mistake, but they aren't thinking right.

Later, Jesus will predict his death and again this will plant more seeds to kill the son. No one has ever resurrected from the dead. This will be the perfect solution.

Remember Jesus is without sin. This gives God the Father the authority to come down and give Jesus back his life by filling him again with the Holy Spirit of God. Now the Holy Spirit, eternal life, that death has no power against, raises Jesus back to life. That is why he is alive, and he can transfer his righteousness to other believers.

You have to understand that I gave him my sin, and he gave me his right standing with God. So when I would say, I am in Christ, it meant that I stand redeemed by the blood that was shed for my sins, and the spiritual life he put inside of me quickened my mortal body and made me come alive spiritually to be able to communicate to the Father through the Son by the Holy Spirit. There is no forgiveness of sin without the shedding of blood.

There was a song about the Father giving the Son and the Son gave the Spirit, and the Spirit gave the Son, and the Son gave the Father. It was called, *And the Gift Goes on*. It did a wonderful job of explaining to me the Trinity of God. It was the Holy Spirit who called to me to come to the Father. Jesus said you can only come to the Father through me. You need my sacrificial life and my righteousness to enter into the Father's realm. They were all working together to get me to the Father.

Wow! He did all that when I first believed. I was born again when I believed. I was filled with the life of Jesus. It had taken me years of following him to come to this revelation where it was mine. Continual revelations of the salvation experience are being revealed each time the gospel is preached. One more piece of the puzzle is put into place. You hear people preaching the gospel. We cannot comprehend or grow from it if we do not apply it to our spiritual lives. I remember; I was always wanting to know more about the resurrection. There were some more powerful truths to learn later in life. That was so powerful and started my spiritual journey into deeper waters.

Jesus defeated Satan and he took his authority away. The bible says that Jesus took the keys away from Satan. Jesus defeated Death, Hell and the grave. Satan had the power to kill humans, now Jesus had that power, and he also had the power to give them his eternal life if they would believe on Him. So, he defeated death with his eternal life.

Another piece of armor is the belt of truth. I could go all day about the truth of God. Throughout this entire book, I am proclaiming the truth of God. I am also using my spiritual shoes. They are how I transport the gospel message of God to others. My feet are also shod with the truth.

Now on my belt is a weapon called the sword of the spirit. That is the word of God. It is the entire truth about God's realm and how he operates his kingdom. The sword is used against the lies of the enemy. It is a defensive and offensive weapon for the believer. All these pieces work together in unity with the word of God.

Jesus claims that we need to learn how to use the words of God in every situation we face in life. We must prove ourselves knowledgeable of the word. Correctly handling the word of God and showing ourselves approved by God.

When I started studying the Psalms carefully I could see there was a court in Heaven. I saw that the spirits are aware of this judgment court too. They know that if God says judgment on them they will suffer terribly. When I realized that Jesus while here on earth used this authority in the spiritual realm then it made perfectly good sense why the demons responded to Him the way they did. He had the power and the authority to call out judgment if they did not obey him at all times. When Jeus commanded they obeyed because they knew who he was. They had to flee when he said so. They had to leave the humans they were inflicting pain and suffering upon. Everywhere that Jesus walked he brought the kingdom of God. All spirits acknowledged and trembled in his presence. Jesus had the ability given to Him by His Father in Heaven to call them into judgment if they refused or stalled to his testmands.

I got to thinking about that. He said he had given his power and authority to us. To his army of spiritual soldiers, we were given this truth. Did we know how to operate in these spiritual abilities was a new challenge. I cannot say that I know all in this department, but I have seen it work on several occasions. Just remember, when you decide to fight the enemy, make sure you are wearing your robe of righteousness and be guilty of nothing in your life that the enemy can accuse you of. If there is a weakness or an infirmity, then he can take you to the judge instead.

Growing in Faith

I found out my faith has different levels. It is like a pond you wade into, and it covers your feet. Then you step out a little deeper, and now the water is up to your ankles. These levels are constantly changing, as we expand our faith in believing that Jesus is alive, and he wants to change us or mold us into his image.

This is the spiritual journey; we all take if we are following Jesus. Sometimes it would seem like I was really getting into deep waters and surely, I would drown if I went any further. You must give yourself time to acclimate to your level. It requires each new truth to be accepted and incorporated into your life. These things take time.

While I was reading my Bible out loud, all the way to the book of Deuteronomy, I heard the voice of God speaking in the scriptures. I could hear him speaking to me as He was speaking to the Israelites, his people. I was now under so much consecration and desire for God, that I was responding with the words they were using. I was seeing the deliverance of the Israelite as my deliverance. My salvation experience was their deliverance from their enemies.

When I read the Psalms, it made perfect sense. I now understand its messages. Because I have read the bible several times in my life, I can transfer from one book to another and easily find the information that I am seeking. It is very common for me to read and study for hours at a time. I do not know how anybody can grow very strong spiritually with just reading a little devotional book every once in a while. If you are truly serious about God and Jesus, then you will study to show yourself a knowledgeable believer. Devotionals have their place in our spiritual walk, but nothing replaces the power of the Bible itself.

Spiritually the typology of scriptures is teaching the reader about God's kingdom and the operation of that kingdom. Like the Israelites, we have come out of Egypt, the world system. The pharaoh in our life was Satan. God delivered us from his hand and power. Just as the Israelites went through the Red Sea, we, his people, must enter into God's realm by being immersed in his spirit. He has to take us through the wilderness to humble us, test us, and teach us to obey his commandments. He says he wants our fellowship, but there are certain things we must know about our God and how he operates when dealing with humans. When we learn these valuable lessons, learn to fear his wrath, and follow his voice, we too will be taken to the promise land. This process is called sanctification in the church vocabulary.

Many people disagree with what is the promise land typology. Many say that it is Heaven. I think it is the kingdom realm of God. Remember there are giants to overcome in the promised land. There is land to be conquered and inhabited. This place is a place to make God your king and live in his realm enjoying all the blessings and avoiding all the curses by obeying the word of God.

I really have a problem with songs that talk about crossing the Jordan River is about dying. I realize they are using it as symbolism. But never was the crossing of the Jordan referred to death. When the Israelites crossed it was to enter into the promise land. There were giants in this new land that God was giving to them to possess. There are no giants to overcome in Heaven.

Now the Greeks and Romans theories were about death, and they had the River Styx. There was a crossing of this river, and a journey was undertaken to pass to the other side. The coins were placed on the eyes to pay the keeeper of the passage way entrance fee. To mix Christianity and pagan beliefs is offensive to me. When these songs are played, I just think they do not know the true word of God. They are singing about traditions and not truths. In fact, there are lots of songs in the Christian church that are wrong biblically. When we sing these songs in the congregation, I just change the words and continue to exalt and glorify God with the truth.

Purification

You will also need to be purified. That means the heat will be applied, and you will be melted down like gold or silver. You will then have the waste products removed, and then you will be pure. That is going to be an ongoing project for the rest of your life. Never will you be proclaimed perfected. You will always be in the process of purification. You will need it forever. The process can be painful, but it is necessary to make you into a vessel that can be used by the Lord your God. He can only truly speak through a vessel that has endured the process and been reprocessed. He wants you to reflect his image in the end.

They call it a metamorphosis process. They use the butterfly as a picture story. When I went to a butterfly farm on one of my many travels, I learned that during the cocoon phase, the larva becomes a liquid, all its body parts liquify and transform into the body of a butterfly with wings. You see, I thought the larva was the body of the butterfly, and he just grew some wings. No, he is truly changed. All the matter and atoms are rearranged, and a new creature emerges.

That is what happens to a Christian if they will allow God to transform them, too. It takes a lot of time and determination to remain faithful in the process. But God will reform you. He will give you a new heart. He will give you a new name. He will transform your mind. He will make you into a new creation. You are no longer a human whose future is judgment. You are now a part of a new first-born creation ready to speak and act on God's behalf. Someone whom He will call friend. You are now a son of God. You are now his chosen one. You are now his priest who represents him in this fallen world.

So, the hay and chaff have to go. The weeds, sticks and stubble have to go. The bad fruit must go. All must be burned up in his consuming fire until the dross is gone. Until we come out like silver and gold. This burning produces ashes. He says he gives beauty for ashes. Another exchange is made. God takes away the parts of life that are unproductive and replaces them with his idea of what is beautiful in a person. What makes a human beautiful to God? Someone who is producing good fruit in their life. Someone who is being a servant to God. Someone who is being a priest to God.

One of my favorite teachings is that Jesus says he is the vine, and I am the branch. I have this saying on several of my decor pieces in my home. I am expected by God to produce good fruit. God likes to use grapes for his symbol of fruit. This fruit makes a nice wine. Well in spiritual language, the wine is the Holy Spirit. So, a vessel holds the wine. That is my body with Jesus living inside of me. This wine is from God, and it has special properties and abilities. The Holy Spirit is my teacher, comforter, encourager, and my correction officer. He wants me to produce good fruit on my vine. God is looking for a good fruit harvest. He wants his grapes full and juicy. He wants for us as Christians to be able to give a glass of Jesus to others from our vessel. Speak the words of God into someone else's life. Remember, we are priests for God, and we represent God to others. We are also living epistles or letters from God to be read to others.

Remember, Christianity is a process. It takes a long time to mature a Christian where they can correctly handle the word of God. Reading and saying what the scripture says about the growth of a Christian is different from experiencing the transformation itself. A child of God knows what he has endured and has been taught over the years. He knows how doubt and disbelief have been replaced with hope and faith. When we read in Revelation about the overcomer, we realize that we too must become an overcomer of the flesh and allow God to make us overcomers too. There are some wonderful promises from God for those who become the overcomer.

Confession with the Mouth

I think, when we realize how our sin hurts us and others the way God sees it, then we will gladly come into agreement with God about how wicked we are to do such terrible things to others. I think it is as simple as telling the truth about the event and to stop lying. God says that all men, that means all the species of human beings on this earth, are all liars. That means they do not and cannot tell the truth about anything sometime in their life. We all lie. The bible says so. Little lies, big lies it does not matter the size, they are all sins in God's eyes, and they need cleansing.

Confession of the wrongs we have committed and getting God's forgiveness extended makes us feel so much better; we are ready to take it to the next level. We are forgiven and God has extended his grace and mercy towards us. We are no longer guilty of performing these sinful acts and behaviors. Now we must see why God said it was wrong in the first place. Why was it a sin?

As we read in the bible, he lists for us several times in the bible lists of sinful behaviors that will need confessing and forgiveness. We call this getting right with God. We allow God to examine our deep issues inside our hearts, and He helps us deal with them, so they will no longer have a negative impact upon our lives anymore. Then we must repent of these sins. That means to never repeat them again in our lives. This takes a lot more work than the confession. Turn around and go the other way. Avoid the traps of sin and do not fall to the temptation again. True repentance will help us to not repeat these familiar sins.

Truth

In prayer we must be truthful to God about our problems, wiring, and reactions to all the circumstances in life we have faced. God is truth. He will not lie to us, and he expects us, when we are in his presence, to be truthful also. Who could be at the throne of God and have the audacity to try to lie to God about our motives. He was there when we made the decision. He knows what our motive was. He just wants us to come to Him. He wants us to come to know him and come over to his side. He wants us to stop playing games and to get real with him. After all, he has chosen to reveal himself to you for a reason and purpose. You are supposed to respond to this revelation.

Once you come to truly realize that the true and living God is listening to you; it will start to change you more and more. They have a word in the religion department; it is called the sanctification process. For me, it has taken my entire life to go through this process. I am still going and will be until the day I die. Being changed from the inside out. Slowly and deliberately, God will have his way in your life. You get to choose if it will be willingly, or you kicking and screaming all the way. Me, I would rather cooperate with the process, allow him his Lordship, and follow him obediently.

But even though I said I will allow Lordship; little did I know how much I would have to change. I was just starting out on the journey of a lifetime. I had escaped Satan and made God my God. He had delivered me from a few works of the flesh. I had responded with thankfulness and given his praise for this mighty work. I had decided to trust him and give him all my sins for forgiveness. And then he gave me one of his greatest gifts of all. He gave me his righteousness.

The Gospel Message

Over the years, I have come to understand this term better. Righteousness, to be in right standing with God. That means you are forgiven for all your sins, and you have been clothed in this robe of white he speaks of in the bible. This covering is pure in God's eyes. This robe allows you to approach the living God without being consumed in his holy fire. The fire will purify you, but it will not destroy you. If you had tried to reach this holy place before you had a robe issued to you, his holy fire would have consumed you.

God cannot be in the presence of sin. Sin is disobeying the rules that God set into effect to continue the operation of the earth. These rules govern the creation and allow for the creatures of creation to know and fellowship with their God. Sin blocks the communication and transmission of thoughts and ideas to and from one another. God wants the channel open. He wants a direct line to us.

Sin blocks the transmission. So, God had to fix the problem. He had to reprogram the human not to sin. How would he accomplish that? They were made in his image, but they were flawed. They needed a Saviour to take away their sins. God needed to get rid of sin and its effects on his creation. He came up with the most elaborate plan that we call the gospel. God put his plan into motion and began making a way for this to be accomplished. That's what Jesus and his story is all about. It tells us about how God did the work to redeem mankind, so they could fellowship with him without being destroyed.

This plan that God devised was perfect and well thought out. It was planned from the beginning and the way was made possible for Jesus to become a human being at the right time in history. God had all the conditions met. He was fulfilling all the prophecies spoken about him in the scriptures. He was arriving on the scene as promised by the prophets. Jesus was the perfect human being. Now the plan was to get Satan to fall for this decoy and actually kill the son of God. The scriptures read that if they had known, they never would have done it.

But they, evil entities, didn't know the entire plan. Jesus and the Father knew the plan. They were in total agreement with one another on how to complete the salvation of human beings. It was a wonderful plan.

First of all, Jesus would have to lay down his life voluntarily. God would pour out all of his wrath on Jesus for all the sins of the world. In the garden before the trails and beatings begin Jesus is praying to God to take the cup away. If there was any other way to save the world. He finally says your will be done and agrees to drink the cup. Now if you read a lot of Bible you will understand this passage better. In different places God refers to the cup. We find after careful study that the cup is God's wrath. Once a person drinks from this cup, it will not stop until it is completely empty. This cup of wrath was what Jesus was sweating blood about. He knew what was in the cup. He did it willingly. He said let it begin. So, the whips and the lashes were all part of the wrath of God upon the flesh of Jesus to finally ending in the cross itself. So, think about it. Jesus endured the wrath a much longer time than we think. So, when the scriptures claim that by his stripes we are healed they are referring to these punishments for sins that Jesus endured. God would throw all his judgments for sin upon Jesus's flesh. Jesus would pay the price for all sins. Jesus would die in the place of all human beings. Jesus referred to this substitution plan when He spoke of the blood of Abel crying out to him. He was redeeming all of his creation. Satan would try to take Jesus to the grave, and then it would all be reversed. It was a perfectly executed plan that ended in a resurrection of the dead. Glory to God; he raised his son back to life. Jesus would take all the power away from Satan, and he would devise a way, by faith, for anyone who would believe could access his new covenant made with God.

The bible claims that Jesus dethroned and removed the weapons that Satan used to take humanity captive and imprison them. Can you think of all the weapons Satan uses to lie, cheat, connive, deceive, kill, and destroy humans? All his weapons have been removed and cannot be used on a believer. Satan is defeated by Jesus. The bible says that Jesus took the keys to death, Hell, and the grave. They now belong to Jesus.

The Garden Parable

While I was learning about God in my bible studies, I had the most wonderful experience in real life that helped to anchor the teachings I was learning in my spiritual life. One day, I decided to weed my garden. I had always desired a pretty entrance garden to set off the house. I knew it was a necessary chore that must be done on a regular basis. I approached the garden determined to execute this chore to the best of my ability. I remembered a long time ago; I had watched my mother painfully pull weeds. She had once tried to teach me, but I was not in the slightest bit interested in doing so or learning how. So, I would say, I flunked weeding 101. Now it was my turn to attempt this daunting task.

First of all, what does a weed look like? I thought to myself, if it is in the grass lawn and in the garden too, then it must be a weed. Therefore, it will be safe to pull these. Also, if I didn't plant it on purpose; it is probably a weed also. But some flower beginnings look like weeds. I don't' want to pull the wrong thing. After all, I planted some seeds a while back, maybe these are the plants just now sprouting. Who knows?

So, I proceeded to pull and pull. That was hard. The weeds were stuck in the ground deep, and they were not budging. I was just managing to take the tops off. That would be no good, they are just going to grow back quickly, and all my hard work will be wasted. Who wants to pull weeds for hours, and it's worth nothing.

I thought about how to make my life easier and less work for me. I thought about why mankind invents different devices to make work easier, and I wondered what new tool could I use? I thought about the hoe, the oldest tool available to mankind, but I did not have good control over where it slashed and dug. I felt for sure that I would end up killing more of the good than the bad. No, this job would require me deciding and then removing the weed without destroying the good plants.

This little truth that I was experiencing became a spiritual moment in my life journey. I had read that God was like the gardener, and my life was his garden. It was his job to remove weeds in my life that were not needed. Some weeds steal the life from the other plants. They compete for the water, sun, and nutrients in the soil. The weeds of my life were doing the same. They were stealing from me the peace of God and the Joy of the Spirit. I thought about how God says that he will harvest the wheat and the tares. He teaches in the Bible that the word of God is the seed that he plants in our heart. Weeds come to steal, kill, and destroy the life God has given us. They come to steal the good that God has planted in us.

The lies that are whispered to us to doubt and disbelieve God's promises, seem to be constantly bombarding our brains. They want us to deny our belief in Jesus being alive. They want us to calm down and not go so overboard with this religion thing. We don't have to believe it literally; that's a crazy man talking. The reality of the world knows better and so do you. Just stop putting all your faith in this Bible stuff. Lay off. God is not really talking to you. And you are not talking to him. This is nuts; stop listening to all these preachers on the radio. Who do you think you are? The voices are constant. They are attacks from my mind, repeatedly telling me to not believe.

The bible said that a double minded believer will receive nothing spiritually. That means that my prayers are not to be expected to be answered. My communication with God will be hindered. Double minded will get you nowhere. Some Christians call it being on the fence. That means you live on the border of the world and God's kingdom. You think you can just hop on to the other side as you please. No, you must be in faith one hundred percent. We need to nail down our disbelief and take it to the cross and give it to Jesus.

But I must believe in Jesus. Jesus himself came to me, and he introduced himself to me. He made it clear, and then he asked me to believe in him.

Now in our lives, we produce some fruit that is not what God would call good fruit. We are still learning. These products come from our flesh. These are not inspired by God. The fruit it produces is worth nothing in God's book, and it must be dealt with. God likes gold and silver, the other, which he calls wood, hay, and stubble must be disposed of properly. Thus, he carefully removes it from our lives, if we will allow him to, and burns it with his purifying power. Bye- Bye bad harvest. That stuff is removed and replaced with the plant that will produce a good fruit in our lives.

So back to weeding. I left the task undone to return to later. Meanwhile, it rained for a few days. So finally, when the rain had stopped, I went back out to start this horrible weeding process again. This time the weeds, when I grabbed them from the base of the plant, came up so easily root and all. I was amazed and grateful for the rain. The plant had been loosened from the soil. Now the whole plant with its root system was being removed. These piles of weeds would be left in the sun without a connection to the soil. They would wither and die. Then they would be piled up to be taken away to the garbage. If burning outside was allowed, then I would have burned them also.

I thought about God and his instructions in my life. Here was a perfect example of how God would take a Christian and fill him with his Spirit. This was the watering. Going to church and worshipping God helps us to be pliable to God. He waters us in his anointings.

Then, he removes the stubborn weeds, root and all. We are willing and obedient to his word, because we have been basking in his goodness during his services. It is like a spiritual surgery. Now the anesthetic has been applied. It does not hurt when he pulls the weeds. We do not fight him about the procedure. In fact, we are willing to allow this surgery to happen. Because we know it is for our own good. There are so many things, thoughts, feelings and emotions that we need to let God deal with. By bringing our needs and hopes to God, this gives him the permission he needs to operate in our lives. When our will matches his will, then he can perform his great works in us and others.

Let us go back to weeding the garden. We have established that God is the gardener in our lives. He knows what weeds are. He says if he did not plant it in you, then it is a weed that needs to be dealt with. He is a gentle farmer caring about every plant in his kingdom. He waters and provides the sunshine for our growth. We are to sink our roots deep into his words of life and expect to grow into a wonderful tree, when the process is completed. Now I am no longer a small plant, but I will mature into a tree. But if I do not take care of the soil, and I allow other plants to invade my territory, then I will not grow strong in God's kingdom, and I will have to suffer with these other plants stealing from me and my nutritional needs.

In one of Jesus's parables, he talks about a sick tree that is not looking very good. He says that the ax will be applied to cut down the tree. The man intervenes he is a gardener and claims that he can help the tree. He says that the ax is not needed. He will just work on the roots and the soil for nutrition around the tree, and it will get better. This is another good example of how we are the plants in God's garden.

Doubts

Can you imagine holding on to the past life and allowing it to continually take what you need to live a clean life? Jesus said he wanted to be Lord over everything. If we hold something back from his dominion, then he cannot provide for all our needs, because we will not let him. We are our worst enemy. So, if you listen to doubt and disbelief, then God considers you a double minded person, and you will receive nothing spiritually in the kingdom of God.

You cannot be on the fence; You cannot choose when and where you will believe. You are either in all the way, or you are out. That is why it is so important to nail this salvation from Jesus down inside your inner core. You have to know, that you know, that you know, that Jesus is alive, and it was God, the creator, who raised Jesus from the dead.

Doubting the validity of the word of God can steal all of your spiritual power and strength. Satan does not want a believer to become obedient, servant of God. In this position the believer is stronger than the enemy because he allows Christ, the victor, to fight the battles.

When we doubt; we call God a liar and say we do not believe him. Satan loves for you to get all tied up in his schemes. His purpose is to tear the believer away from his faith. This opens the door to fear. The enemy will use fear to paralyze a believer. They will be unable to function if they give a place for doubt to remain.

The Light of God

References to the light of God are throughout the bible. In the beginning, the book of Genesis, God said, "Let there be light." And God created the earth. One of Jesus's titles is he is the light. When we refer to the fight between good and evil we use light and darkness as symbols to represent the spiritual concepts. The light disperses the darkness. It overcomes the darkness. People, who are hiding from God, walk in darkness. That means they are blind to the truth about God. They stumble in the dark. While serving the evil one in life, it is said we walk and stumble in the darkness. The bible says that the sinners hate the light because it exposes their sins. They prefer the darkness where they can behave wrongly and not be seen. Of course they can be seen. God sees everything. There is nowhere on this planet you can go and hide from God.

Christians welcome the light. It shines on their pathway and gives them direction in life. It illuminates the dark corners of our life and helps us find the hidden truths that can hinder our lives. The light symbolizes the enlightening process of the mind. In God's words the light opens up a believer to learn and understand spiritual truths.

The believer comes to realize that the only way he can overcome himself and the evil one is to make God their God. They will need to humble themselves before God, die to their fleshly sinful desires, agree with the will of God, and realize only by submitting to God will we survive this world's influence.

Response to Gospel

Many a human hears the plan of salvation and rejects it. Others believe and respond with thankfulness and curiosity. Others, their response is also genuine, but they are so busy with other things in life that they just dismiss the entire matter and let it simmer on the back burner their entire lives.

Then, there are the few who realize that the gift they have been given is like the pearl of great value. It is worth everything and is more valuable than their life. They pursue God, and they sit at his feet to learn of him. They make him Lord of their life and commit for a lifetime that God will be their God forever. Nothing is more important in their lives than God, Jesus, and the Holy Spirit.

These responses are the ones the bible talks about when it says the seed fell in good soil. I prayed when I read this parable that I would be good soil. My heart is the earth where the seed is planted. My heart, my love for God, is all consuming, it is my main purpose of life. When people ask me what are you passionate about? I say; "I am passionate about God and his plan of salvation."

God wrote his spiritual laws upon my heart. The bible refers to this as circumcision of the heart. The Ten
Commandments were called the law of God. Now these are the spiritual laws for a believer to live daily. God said He is God and there are no other Gods before him. He said I must love him with all my heart, strength, might, and power. That means everything I have got inside of me, all purposes, goals, plans, vigor they all go to God. If I love something more than God, then I have made a little 'g' god out of that person or object. It is a tall order. It requires sacrifices on the believer's part to

obey the commands of God. But in the end, it is worth it all. Obedience is better than sacrifice the scriptures read.

Dealing with Sin

He saved a wretch like me. I knew I was a wretch. I agreed to that easily. But some of the other sins of the flesh, I struggled with and tried to skirt around them. I would try to read around it and say that is not what that means. I would table that sin and deal with some others. But it would always come back to the sins of the flesh. God in his mercy would deal with me, over and over again, over the years. I would tell him I was trying, but it was too hard. I was not capable, but he showed me my problem.

I was playing God and deciding what was a sin and what was not. God said he decides. I was saying, I will decide. Then the question became, is your God really God or not? How can you claim him and still disobey? You are a hypocrite. You claim; he is your God. You go to church and exalt his name. You sing to him and claim you are his child, but yet you do not obey. The words of Jesus ringing in my ears. "If you love me, obey my commands."

I would argue that was not a command. It was just something Paul said, and he was just a man. Then in my face Jesus, in the gospels, he speaks of it also. No, my flesh screamed; we cannot do this. My spirit cries; we have to obey. I cannot live without the living God in my life. I cannot go back to my lost position where I dwelled in darkness. I do not want to live that way ever again.

Jesus talking to the woman at the well. He says go and sin no more after he heals her by speaking to her spirit. Oh dear, these words are killers. I am the woman at the well. I have had many a man sexually, because the world has argued that two consenting adults can do what they please. No one should make them feel guilty. Oh well, I do feel guilty.

Now God is dealing with this behavior in my life. He wants to clean me up in all departments. I have confessed all these sins, and now there are more I must deal with. Oh, this is a big can of worms that I do not want to deal with. Hey God, can't we just leave this one alone and pretend we are doing everything correctly? Can't you just turn your head and act like you do not see the problem? Will this sin cause me to stop growing in the spirit? Will I cease to be able to hear the spirit speak to me so sweetly? Where will my guide be? What about his presence; will he pull away? I am a stinking sinner. I am just as bad as everyone else. I am hopeless. Leave me alone God; I am not worthy. I am a failure in this Christianity Walk.

Disbelief

These are my thoughts, but they are also being driven by another evil force that is condemning me too. He is saying, that is right; God expects too much. Nobody can live like that. See that is what happens when you try to live the bible. It is impossible. Go ahead, give up and return to your old life and lies. You gave it a good shot. It is ok, everybody else had to deal with these problems and look where they are today. It is ok to disobey God in this one department. After all, that was written 2,000 years ago; no one expects you to literally apply all of this bible rubbish to your life today. Grow up and take control of your life.

Lies of the evil one, Satan, are damaging to a Christian, if we accept them as our own. You know a long time ago, they told little boys if they do wrong, lightning would strike them dead. Well, they did wrong and survived. We did wrong and survived. So, we learned the wrong lesson. We said there was no judgment. Nothing is going to happen to us if we do wrong. That is just an old wives' tale. Well over the years, I have seen it proven in life that there is a reaping for the sins of the flesh that we sow today. We may not be able to associate the judgment matching which particular sin, but we definitely experience some, horrific events in life that could be given credit as judgment. No one likes to think that there is that side of God. But there definitely is, and he will use it to get our attention.

Over the years, we saw many public preachers and evangelists fall to the sexual impurity behaviors. It ruined their ministries, and I think to myself they, too, wrestled against those same thoughts I had. They made the mistake and compromised. They continued in their sins and the reaping was the whirlwind. It was a terrible crash. They represented the bible to the world, and their sins tarnished the message they had preached for so long. God's kingdom suffered a blow. The gospel message was jeopardized. People who had followed these preachers were now shaken to their foundations. They had believed the preacher. Maybe they had not read it for themselves. Maybe this forced them to have to deal with their own lives and behaviors. Whatever the reasons for the falls, it had many different impacts on believers and non- believers throughout the world.

Marriage

Once again, I would have to deal with my own behaviors in sexual immorality and its definitions. I was divorced during this time. I was not even thinking of ever remarrying. Then God dropped into my spirit that he wanted me to remarry again. I said absolutely not. I was not going to give a man control over my life again. I was very happy the way I was and did not need a husband. He explained that a husband who was a Christian would be different. He would be under Jesus's domain and would be able to love me as Christ loved the church. There should be no problem submitting to a man like that, because he would have Jesus inside of him, and I could trust the Lord. It made sense, so I agreed to the idea of remarrying. I read scriptures about if it was even possible for me. I had already tried to reconcile with my first husband after I got saved, because that was what the scripture said to do. According to scriptures, it appeared to me, I was allowed to remarry, but I must marry a believer this time and not be unevenly yoked. I accepted the command and became willing to consider the possibility.

Cults

What was happening to me? I was becoming a Jesus freak. I was reading my bible all the time. I was finally getting some of the big pictures of what was occurring in the Old Testament and how this was influencing me as a believer. But I was worried. I thought I do not want to end up like those crazy people I had seen riding a bicycle with posters filled with scriptures warning people plastered all over the bike. I did not want to be that crazy person driving a van with scriptures painted all over it. I did not want to be labeled crazy or insane. I wanted to know and understand the scriptures spiritually and to know the difference in lies of religions and Christianity.

My brain was attacking me and saying that I belonged to a cult. That I was in over my head, and I was becoming another victim of too much zeal for religion. I decided to study all the different religions and their foundational belief systems. I needed to know their basic viewpoints about Jesus. That would determine for me if they were or were not a cult.

The bible had said that no man can come to the Father except through Jesus. If they were attempting to worship God and ignoring Jesus, then I put them on my cult list. If they were claiming other lies about who God is and in direct opposition to the Bible, they also went on the list. Some of them, I had to study deeper to find the errors in their teachings. But once they were exposed, they too went on the cult side.

By practicing this method, it gave me more confidence in myself that the Jesus I had believed in, was definitely the correct one. I was not in any way, at all, following a cult. In fact, I was extremely biblical in my denomination that I was attending. By studying the cults, I built my foundation even stronger in Jesus.

Now I am not here to throw stones at anyone else's religion, but there were different theories I researched to determine how they stood according to the Bible. I do not want to be a basher of religion, and I will try to tread lightly in this department.

The first one I studied were the Mormons. My husband and I were planning a trip to Utah so, naturally, I wanted to investigate what to expect while we were there. Naturally while we were there, we explored the Mormon Tabernacle where the famous Mormon choir sings the Hallelujah Chorus. We visited several museums which contained the personal belongings of the early Mormons who had crossed the continent to settle there and establish their own denomination. They were also known as the beehive state because they were always busy getting things done.

Now they call themselves Christian, claim they are born again, and are in the body of Christ. Therefore, I had to look very closely at their ceremonies, actions, and beliefs to determine if they were truly Christian. I learned so many disturbing aspects about their quests that they follow.

It seems that they must get married in the temple. During this ceremony, the wife will receive her new name that her husband will use to call her up to him when he resurrects. If he does not call her, then she is just left and has no recourse.

It appears the men believe that they too, will be like God and go off and create their own earths and make their own garden of Eden type experiences. This means they believe they are little gods in training. Now this was a little weird for me to understand. But as I read more books on the subject, I realized that was the problem.

They believe our God, the creator and the author of the Bible, was once a man who also acquired godhead status. Whoa, that is not what the Bible teaches. God is not an exalted human. He is so much more than that.

These early Mormon settlers believe they are going to become a god like my God. I don't think so. All of those personal possessions in that museum are because they think these predecessors of theirs were like little gods. So, they have their hair combs, their toothbrushes, their personal toiletry items saved because they belong to the gods.

Then I discovered that the totally devoted Mormon wear some kind of undergarment for the rest of their life, and they never remove it entirely. It's like they think it is their robe of righteousness which is given to the believer by God as a spiritual covering. I am sorry, but this religion was placed into the cult side. If you don't have the right God, then you can't have the right Jesus either.

The next religion I decided to try to understand was the Hindu religion. I knew it was the big question of reincarnation that I was seeking truth about. I found that the strong believers in reincarnation are seeking a way to break the cycle that they are doomed to keep performing. I learned that they say the mantra repeatedly to help them escape reincarnation. You see they are looking to reach a Nirvana stage. This will free them. So, they empty their mind and concentrate on the mantra seeking to rid themselves of this cycle.

I thought to myself how silly this sounds. The power of resurrection from the dead breaks the reincarnation cycle. The scriptures tell us that we live, we die, and then the judgment. There is no over and over again trying to live better every time you return to earth to live again. It is really sad when you think about how many people in the world are in bondage, because they have accepted this belief as a truth.

So next were the Jehovah Witness crowd. After reading some of their material, it was very clear to me that I needed to stay away from their beliefs. First of all, in their beliefs, Jesus was not God. If Jesus is not God, then how can I worship him I questioned? I do worship Him. Jesus said if you have seen me, you have seen the Father. He said he only does what the Father does, says or thinks. I believe Jesus is God who took on human form. He left his divinity as the Father in Heaven. Jesus, as the human form, will be forever that form, but he is still the word of God. He sits at the right hand of the Father. This is the trinity concept and obviously the Jehovah Witnesses did not believe any of that. They were having to work to prove they were worthy for God. That was sad, because Jesus is the one that makes us worthy of the Father.

Then there were the secret societies, like the Masons and the Shriners, that meet in different buildings and have some very strange rituals. I would most likely call it Satanism, because it definitely is not God centered. The name of Jesus is forbidden so that is enough for me.

Roman Catholic Church

Now I don't want to be accused of being an anti anything. The following and the previous accusations are not just based out of thin air. I spent years researching and re-researching these premises before I concluded anything at all. If any of this makes you angry or uncomfortable, then I suggest you seek out your own answers.

You can write your own personal testimony too. Readers, I have to write the way I learned it. What I have learned over the last four decades of following my Jesus. I take all of this task extremely seriously, and I can back up my words with evidence.

The next denomination that I was to study was a big one. The Roman Catholic Church and all of its teachings would take me years of study. Wow! How could I be so wrong? My first big encounter was at a Holy Ghost Conference in New Orleans. This was during the big Charismatic movements in the churches, and even the Catholic churches were experiencing this revival.

We were all in a large arena listening to a very powerful, famous preacher, and he gave an altar call. All the Catholics stood up. He had asked who would like to receive Jesus as their savior today. To the Catholics this meant to receive communion rites. They were all reseated and asked again in another way about the salvation question. Several still stood up and wanted to ask Jesus into their life. It was sad to me, because the Catholic leaders took that group of Catholics, and the rest went to a different room. I saw many wearing Jesus buttons, but above his image was the Virgin Mary button also. This was my beginning into my investigations that I would pursue for the next twenty years.

Jesus is the only one who deserves my worship. No one else died for my sins. No one else took my judgment for my sins. No one, but Jesus. He was raised from the dead by the Father because of his righteousness. Just because a vessel carries a holy thing, that does not mean the vessel is holy also. There is no power in the vessel, unless the living holy entity moves through that vessel.

These are some of the truths that will need to be applied to the following misinformation or doctrines of the church. Sacred cows are what I call them. They are to be left alone and not referred to or discussed in any unholy manner. So, am I just supposed to ignore these things and shake my head in agreement? This unsaid agreement will doom millions to their fates of following idolatrous idols? I have seen the churches and the statues. I have pictures of the statues that are paraded in the streets, while the whole town shuts down business to engage in the frivolities of the man-made, holy, holiday, worship ceremonies. It reminds me of when Moses came down from the mountain and witnessed everybody dancing and partying around the golden calf. It was idol worship back then, and it is still that today. No matter how you try to disguise it.

Yes, there are many Christians in that denomination, but the things that they are taught hamper their spiritual journey instead of helping. Now I must tread lightly in these areas. I realize in the olden times, what I am going to write would be considered heresy and enough reason to cause my death. Thank God, times are a little better, and there is still freedom of speech.

The biggest stumbling block I think the Catholic church adds to the believer's burden is the concept of Mary the mother of Jesus. Their beliefs are hidden, but if you dig deep enough the truth is exposed.

First of all, they believe that not only was Mary a virgin, but she too had an immaculate conception, and she was born of a virgin also. This way she is clean from sins on the mother's side. The Father's side was God, and he was completely without sin. Then they tell the believer that Jesus is too busy or too mean to listen to their prayers. But if they go through Mary, she has Jesus's heart in her hands. She can console Jesus and cause him to listen to your prayers and possibly grant your petitions.

What did I just say? Do I have to pray to Mary to get my prayers answered? What happened to Jesus telling me to pray to the Father in his name to receive my request? He never said I needed another intercessor besides Jesus. It is so simple for the church to throw Mary worship in their services. After all, she is the Mother of God. She is just as important as He is, so they say. I have been to the Catholic Churches around the world, and I have seen the statues they have made to Mary on their altars. They are usually above Jesus and bigger than his statue. They are ladened with gold. They worship an idol. They give her powers she does not possess. There are churches where they worship the milk from her breast. There are other churches where she is supposed to have appeared to believers. It goes on and on.

The Old Testament talked about the worship of a goddess. They called her the Queen of Heaven. So, this is nothing new. Humanity will worship a spirit hiding behind the statue of Mary. Think about how many little statues exist in people's homes. You might even have one too.

When I first entered the body of Christ, as a new believer, I did not know the difference. I embraced this church because it was called the Mother Church. It had kept Christianity through the centuries and preserved the word of God. They were the only church that had the truth. But as I began to study their beliefs, I found so many errors and contradictions to the commands of the Bible.

What is with all the saints? Why would I pray to a dead saint. He is just a human being who found Jesus in his life. Because of his love for God and the infilling of the spirit of God, this man or woman did wonderful works for the kingdom of God. They were just living according to the spirit's leading. They had a living relationship with the Father. Just like every believer in Jesus can have also.

So when you die, do you want us erecting a statue in your name and praying to you to help us in our troubles here on earth? Well, that is exactly what the Catholic church does. Think about it. Because Billy Graham was such a Godly man, we will erect statues to him and pray to him? Does that sound pleasing to God? He warns us, over and over again, in the Bible, do not worship idols. He said do not make a graven image of your little g god. He said they are made of wood or stone and they can not hear you or help you. He is constantly warning about this idolatry worship. In fact, it is what brought the judgment of God upon the northern tribes of Israel. They were warned repeatedly. God finally gave them a certificate of divorce and claimed they were practicing harlotry. He said do not worship other Gods. He said he was the one God, and there was none other. Following idolatry worship is wrong for Bible believers.

Most people are not aware of the other strange customs the Catholic Church practices and believes. There is the rosary and the prayers that accompany it. There are the stations of the cross prayers. Then there is the communion service and the question of transubstantiation. This is where they literally believe the bread and wine become the flesh and the blood of Jesus. It is an heretical view to think this is symbolism.

Another antibiblical behavior was the priests selling absolutions to non believers. Or how about paying the priest enough money or jewels to pray for your dead one to be free from going to Hell or Purgatory. Money can get you all kinds of benefits seems to be the message of the priests. These rites and rituals were blasphemy against God and his plans of salvation. Once you are dead, you don't get to be prayed out of your destination. That is just wrong to tell someone you have the power to do this.

Then there were the relics. These were the items of the dead people who had an anointing while here on earth. If you pay enough to the church, you can kiss the relic, and it will bring you healing and wealth.

Then there are the Church leaders. The idea of a Pope claiming he is God's representative here on earth. He has great political power and acts like he speaks with the authority of God. I have been to the Vatican City. I have seen the churches there. Believe me, I would never kiss that man's ring in submission to his unholy church. That would be to deny my Jesus and the Bible to submit to his rule and dominion.

The Protestant religions developed in protest of the Catholic rituals. This is where our different denominations came from. The bible was finally translated into the common man's language, and they were able to learn what it really said. This was the beginning of the enlightenment period. The word of God brought light to men's souls.

I'm sorry if it sounds harsh. When these religions are unmasked and shown under the light of God there is no way of ignoring these practices. You decide if it is enough to put them on a list.

Bookstore

Now in Georgia, where I was saved, I would visit these wonderful Bible bookstores. The atmosphere was encouraging, they were playing wonderful worship music in the background, and all the products were exalting Jesus. It was very comforting and encouraging to me, when I would visit. You know you have truly made a commitment to Jesus when you put up some plaque in your home proclaiming your new faith

I thought all stores should be the same. When I moved back to Tennessee, I found that was not the case. In the Tennessee's store, I was so disappointed. I felt like I did not even belong in the store. There was no one to fellowship the spirit with, and the atmosphere was dead. I mentioned this in my prayers to God and told him it was a shame that his name was not exalted and glorified in a store like that.

Oh boy, that was a mistake. Naturally, he decides that I should have the honor of representing him with a store. What? I do not know anything about books. I barely read for enjoyment, and the only book worth reading is the Bible. Yes, I have a degree in business, but what do I know about the inside operations of a store?

Later on, I am looking in a Christian magazine, and in the back are the classifieds. There is an advertisement selling tapes on how to own and operate a bookstore. Oh my goodness, you talk about how the Lord will order your steps. Here were the beginning answers to my objections. So, I ordered and listened to the tapes with great enthusiasm. I took notes and made references to where to order products from. It looked like I was going to own and operate a bookstore.

There were two stores already operating in the city. One had been in existence forever. It was not looking for any young female to add her two cents worth of knowledge. The other one was disgusting. The place had books piled on the floor, it looked like a place where the clergy purchased their church supplies, and it was very impersonal. There was no pretty décor to exalt Jesus. There was no worship music playing anywhere. It was very questionable if they were even born-again believer owners. It was spiritually dead inside. It was located in a questionable neighborhood, so I could not understand why God would want me to buy into that. I found out later, it was operated by three men from different churches. Again, would they even allow a female any say so in a place like that. I did not like it. I told the Lord my feelings in prayer and explained my reasoning. As far as I was concerned, it was no longer an option.

So stubborn me went to find her own idea of a place that would be appropriate for this kind of business. Did God direct me? Yes, he did. I found a nice store front and approached the owner. I told him my plans. I had no idea who or what he was, because I was not from this town. He was thrilled and said that would be the only type of business he would consider renting to and would be happy to have me as a tenant. Wow! That was easy. God was definitely leading and ordering in this endeavor.

The next hurdle was fixtures. I would need shelves and displays for the products. I heard that a store downtown had the old fixtures from the Woolworth's store in their attic, and I could get them for a good price. I knew nothing about these things. Metal shelving with pegboard backings put together to form shelves like in a grocery store. Wow again! It was perfect. I had no idea how many I would need. I bought what they had in good shape. I took this home to the house I was renting and began painting all of the units the appropriate color scheme that I had chosen for the store. I had the place carpeted and painted the walls. I had studs attached to the walls, so I could attach wooden shelves that could hold heavy weighted products without collapsing.

Now during all of these preparations, before I was ready to open, the other store, I had considered purchasing, moved to a shopping center and became a really nice place. I thought, oh dear, I am too late. I have dragged my feet, and God has moved on without me. Someone else answered his call. It was then that I realized how much I wanted to open this store for him and his word. It was a recommitment to the ministry call. I realized I wanted to do his will here on earth as it is done in heaven.

Now I was ready to open the store. What was going to be the name of the store. While listening to some preaching on TV, I heard a sermon about the word of God is the absolute word. I thought; I like that, so I named my store, The Absolute Word. I had a location; I had the fixtures, now I needed the product. I knew nothing about what should be in a store. I was so ignorant about authors and book titles that I did not want any books at first. I wanted lots of bibles by every type of publisher. I wanted every kind of translation and version. I wanted a few cute gifts, and some reference books like commentaries and concordances. That was my beginning inventory.

I had set aside $20,000 for investment purposes, and I was approaching my limit quickly. It was a beautiful store with little signs hanging from the ceiling with words of encouragement to the shoppers. I remember one said, Know Who You Are in Jesus.

The store was ready to open. I was so ignorant and naïve. But God had made me bold and brave. I threw myself into this project with all of my love and abilities. It was my sacrifice for God. I loved Jesus, and I wanted to share that with others. Years went by, and the store grew and slowed, and grew again. At one time, I rented the property next door and expanded the store. I finally gave in to books, and we sold a ton of books. I had distributors to get orders quickly, I had music, t-shirts, bibles, gifts and books.

I was only one year old in the faith of Jesus. I had so much to learn. I read and studied my bible all the time. I fellowshipped with other Christians and attended many church services throughout the week. I listened to so much teaching and I was allowing Jesus to transform me into more of his image.

It was a wonderful place. I had hired three ladies to work there. They loved the store as if it was their own. There was a lot of ministry that took place in that store over the years. It was a place where people could come in and fellowship with other Christians and talk about their spiritual walk with Jesus. He was exalted and adored in that place. I was so blessed to have been given the opportunity to serve God like that for the amount of time that I was given.

The End of the Store

But the world raised its ugly head and in the end; I was defeated and had to close the store. I kept it going for ten years. I had poured my own personal money in it for a long time. Finally with overwhelming circumstances, I could not continue to operate the store. I was blessed to find a store that was interested in purchasing my unsold inventory. I got a few cents on the dollar and unloaded the contents of the store.

During the struggles, I learned so many spiritual lessons. The biggest one was that my store was a living entity. I had brought it forth. It was alive. It had its own personality based on the people who attended it. I struggled deep inside to keep it afloat. Sometimes, even when God is in it, it does not always prosper. This is one of the lies of the church world. God was in it. That was clear to me. I had remained in it.

I had so many difficulties occurring in my personal life. God was faithful to me. I was being sifted. I was being purified. I was going through the flames of fire. I was enduring storm after storm. I was devastated, I was ruined, I was defeated. My struggles included a failed marriage, failed business, failed stepfamily relationships, and every other disaster that could happen to me. But my relationship with Jesus held me close to him, and I survived.

End of Marriage #2

After my husband left me for another woman, and I lost my stepchildren whom I had loved as my own, I was left with my two daughters. I knew I would have to provide a living for us, so I returned to college and acquired my teaching degree. I was in my forties, and I was one of the oldest student in class. I brushed off my skills, acquired new ones, and launched into my second career. First, I had to complete courses that were undergraduate requirements for Education. Then I had to pass the Master's entrance exam. After that, I began attending my classes. My mission was to achieve a teacher's license.

I was called to be a teacher way back in my teens, but I had ignored the calling, because I knew teachers did not make a decent wage in life. So now, I am submitting to the calling and working diligently to complete my master's in education. I finally accomplished this by the year 2000.

The Gospel

It was God's idea to become a man in the form of his son. It was his purpose for coming to the earth. He died for the sacrifice of our sins. He did not deserve to die. The wages of sin is death the Bible says. But Jesus never sinned. He was purely righteous in everything he did or said. It was wrong for death to come for him.

Jesus was filled with eternal life. That spirit that lived in Jesus while He was on earth kept him alive. We call it eternal life and Jesus could not be killed by anyone or anything, unless He allowed it.

On the cross, after taking the judgment that God poured out on him for all human beings, he then gave up his Holy Spirit and allowed death to think he had conquered him. But God knew what was going to happen. They had it all planned out. God would give Jesus back his eternal spirit. Satan had overstepped his boundaries. He had taken an innocent man to the grave. This was not allowed. He had broken a spiritual law that even he was governed by himself.

Now Satan lost control of the death and the grave. Jesus took the keys. He took his authority and power over humans away from him. Jesus conquered the grave. He took possession of who would go there and who would not go there.

He made a covenant with God. It would be by faith mankind would be able and allowed to enter God's kingdom. He made a promise to take care of the believers. He said they would not go to the grave; they would belong to him, and he would give them life. He would give them his eternal life if they would just believe that he was alive. The bible says the spirit was given as an earnest payment. That means because the Holy Spirit is in our lives, we know that the rest of God's promises are yes and amen, too.

Jesus claimed he was the door to the Father and his kingdom. He said for all who would believe in him, they would be made alive in the spirit. Their bodies would be quickened by the Holy Spirit, and this is what we call being born again. The spirit of God births us into his life.

Ask any born-again Christian what happened to them when they first believed the message of God. We call that message the gospel. We were changed; we were awakened. We felt alive for the first time in our life. We knew our sins had been forgiven, and it was a release from a prison of sin. We were filled with the Spirit of God and could actually understand spiritual thoughts and ideas for the first time. We had a love for God placed deep inside of our hearts. We could hear the savior's voice, and we knew he loved us. We were delirious with this love of God that was manifesting itself in our lives. We developed a communication with Jesus.

So many things were happening and changing. We did not understand all of it at once. God revealed it to us a little at a time. He did not want to overwhelm our sensory perceptions. He revealed himself gradually. Every time a believer seeks God; he understands a little bit more. Gradually he is growing in Christ.

For me, I wanted to know it all. I wanted to know how it happened. Why did it happen? Who was this God that I was communicating with? Who is this God that I love with all my heart, mind, and strength? Tell me more and more. Help me find out all the truths you, Holy Spirit, will allow me to learn. I will expose myself to this God. Understand that he is not interfering, but he is intervening in my life. He wants to help me become a better person. He says follow me. I say yes Lord, I will follow you for the rest of my life. You have the words of life where else can I go?

People assume that once we ask Jesus into our life, we are supposed to be perfect now. This is not true. We have to allow God to change and mold us into his image. When he first starts with us, we are a mess. He knows how to work on us and reshape us. He asks that we do not stop believing in his gospel message, and that we will turn our lives and control of those lives unto him. I once heard a preacher say God loves us too much to allow us to stay the way we are. He is not leaving us. We remain with him, and he will do his powerful spiritual work in us. That is what it means to allow Christ to live in us.

Remember earlier, I was talking about purification by God. Well, this burning up of the chaff in our lives is very difficult sometimes. Chaff is not good wheat. You can not make good bread for others to feed upon with chaff, so it must be eliminated. It can become quite painful, and the process of purification can be brutal. The scripture says he gives us beauty for our ashes. Ashes are what is left after the burning. To me it means when he is finished the phases of purification at the end of each part there is a beautiful effect observed in the person. God is gradually refining us to become and be used as a vessel for him.

He is never finished with us. God does it in steps. He does not fix us overnight. It took a long time for us to develop wrong values, and it will take a long time to correct our inner being, thoughts, and attitudes. Our character is important to God. He wants us to behave like Jesus behaved. We represent Jesus to the lost person. We represent God to others. They need to see the living and available God in us.

Before we can represent, speak for God, or minister his love and truths, we have to endure the purifying processes over and over again. God wants to use us. The better we are conformed to his image, the stronger our message will become. We will be able to penetrate thick and strong walls of disbelief by yielding to the power of the Holy Spirit that is always abiding in us.

Well of Living Water

The Spirit of God is many times referred to as the water of life. There are so many references in the bible about the water of God. Scriptures themselves are the water. If you are thirsty spiritually read the words of life. We are encouraged to drink from the well of God's spirit. He speaks of watering our souls with the waters of God.

He tells us that we too, have a well inside of us. We too, are filled with the water of God. Our well is life giving to us and others. We can offer another person a drink of this living water. When I speak to people about Godly matters, and they are listening and comprehending spiritually the truths I am talking about, I call that phenomenon drinking from my well. I can tell when someone is drinking. The spirit of God in me speaks to their spirit and quickens them. They are encouraged spiritually. Other scripture talks about having a spiritual ear. Let them hear what the scripture is speaking. All of these references speak of being able to discern and understand what the Holy Spirit is teaching the believer.

There was this great song we learned in the 1980's called "I've Got a River of Life Flowing Out of Me". In the refrain, it would read, spring up ole well, within my soul, spring up ole well and make me whole. Spring up ole well and give to me that life abundantly.

Jesus mentions the well several times. He tells us there is only one well within us. Our spirit brings out the Godly words, and our fleshly nature speaks the world language. He says they both can't operate in our lives. It is up to the believer to decide what will flow from his heart. Will it be life giving water of the waters of sin and death. Only one can flow at a time.

Another talk about the water was when he tells the woman that he has the words of life. He will give her the living water where she will never thirst again. Humans are thirsty for the God part of life. They are empty and shallow and need meaning in their God forsaken, spiritually rotten, dead in their sins lives. They know something is missing. They just don't know or understand what that missing part is. God is the missing part.

How stubborn mankind is. They refuse to drink this water that Jesus died to help them receive. He did all of that by sacrificing his life for them. He wants them to be alive to him. He wants them to be a part of his kingdom. If they will only choose him to be their God, he promises to make their life full of meaning and to bless the believer with his love and attention. The believer is a child of God, and he is highly favored in life here on earth, because he belongs to God. It's a win-win situation. Why do they refuse to believe?

The Role of the Holy Spirit

God sends his spirit out to offer an invitation to any human being who would like to become his child. Most people, like me, do not know the answer to the question he will ask of us. Who is Jesus to you? If you respond, he is my savior and the forgiver of my sins, then he will ask you would you like an audience with this God? Would you like a place at his dining table? He might say, I have been authorized by God himself to go to all of his believers and invite them to his banquet hall. What will be your answer? Will you say yes, I would love to come, or will you tell him you are too busy with life's events and do not have the time? The Spirit of God is always seeking believers and non-believers to accept his invitation.

Let's discuss a non-believer. We in the Christin world call this person a lost soul. A person who is found means they have accepted Jesus into their heart and received his grace giving, eternal life, spirit. Therefore, a lost person is ignorant of Jesus and his ability to save them. Most lost people are not even aware they are lost. Some are under a lot of convictions from their continual sinning. A lost person knows deep down inside something is not right. They know they are missing something in life, but they are not aware or able to put their finger on the problem. Usually, it is not until we are saved, that we can look back and perceive how utterly lost we were.

Non-believers act differently than believers. They speak differently also. Usually, you can recognize one fairly quickly from their different manners and ways of behaving. It is almost like they have a big sign attached to them that declares, "Please, help me I am lost and confused about everything. I need help."

We believers have the obligation to help them find Jesus. They need him just like we did. Telling people is just sharing with them what Jesus has done in your life, and how he can do the same thing for them. We might just plant a seed of hope in their life. We might actually get to lead them in prayer to find Jesus. But anything we do to help is appreciated and pleases God.

What is God's message? He wants to tell them he is not mad at them. He wants to tell them he understands them and can help them, if they will let him. He has the power to extend his grace and forgiveness for all their sins. He wants to be their Father, and they become one of his children. He offers them hope and promises that only God can give. He asks them to believe that he raised his son Jesus from the dead. He wants them to believe in Him, and that he is God.

Wow! Just believe in him, and he will give us his eternal life! Is it really that simple? Yes, it is.

Songs of the Faith

There was a hymn called, "Love Lifted Me". It speaks about how we were in the miry clay sinking to rise no more, God heard our despairing cry, he lifted us out of our mess, and set us on the foundation of Jesus his son. This demonstrates how God rescues a lost person who has been taken captive by the enemy and finds himself locked away in a spiritual prison.

Then there was another song by Andre Crouch. It too was about God lifting us out of our grave and circumstances. Our sin was so strong in our life it held us prisoner. We were so beaten down; we were no longer able to lift our heads in any kind of hope. We could not help ourselves. We were in chains and bondage to the world and its ruler. He was a cruel task master. We were miserable in our lives, and there was no way out that we could see or think of as a possibility. Our chains were strong; no one could break them. Our cells were dark and filled with horrors of the mind. We were tortured inside of our souls. We were lost and undone because we were without God or his son, Jesus.

Then the song says, "When God Reached Down His Hand for Me." He reached way down for me. We would sing this in choir. I would sing this song with all of my heart. Those words were alive and strong. They were echoing exactly how I felt when I was lost and in the pit of despair. My God crashed the gates of Hell and rescued me. He set me free and took all those chains and broke them apart. He delivered me from my addictions. He opened my eyes to the truths about him. He gave me spiritual eyes, and I saw the light of God. The darkness was gone. I had a sane mind. I could lift my head up and gaze upon my God and savior.

He did all this when I first believed. It truly was such a tremendous, glorious miracle when my Savior reached down his hand for me. Can you see and understand why I rejoice all the time? Do you see why I am so grateful for his salvation? He put his spirit inside of me. He set me free from death, Hell, and the grave. He gave me a new life and a new nature. I was no longer a stiff-necked rebellious person. I wanted to show my gratefulness and my love for and to my God forever. I became a worshipper, because I wanted to honor the one who had rescued me.

There are so many scriptures that tell a believer to rejoice in the Lord. So, one day I am worshipping, and I start to contemplate the word rejoice. I think to myself the prefix of the word is re. Re means to do it again. So, I think about the word joice. That comes from the word joy. Oh! I exclaim that makes lots of sense. Rejoice means to find the joy of the Lord again. To rejoice is to stir up the mind and remember what gave you joy in the first place. The spirit directs me to think about my salvation experience, and how joyful I was when I was set free from all of my sins and bad behaviors. You were so full of joy. Rejoice, remember, and recall that joyful feeling. Joyful, that means full of joy. Sometimes, English actually makes sense.

If you keep rejoicing, then you might not lose your first love. Contemplating and meditating on what you know spiritually is another way to grow and learn to hear the voice of God. The scriptures say that a believer can hear the voice of God. I have met so many Christians that will confess they do not know the voice. That is sad for them. They need to return to their salvation birth and recall if they heard the voice back then. Then, they need to retrace their spiritual steps to determine when they stopped listening. God says we have been given a spiritual ear to hear his truths. Sometimes we need to return to our encounter with Jesus and start back at the beginning. Fill in what you have learned and allow the spirit to explain the parts you still do not quite understand.

All Christians need to be able to hear and understand the scriptures spiritually. That is one way that God communicates with His creation. He designed the words to tell all about Him and His desires for us. I encourage every one to read the scriptures aloud and listen for God's voice when He speaks. He is all over the place.

Songs after songs flood my mind. "I Never Shall Forget the Day" speaks of that day in every Christian's life. You can just Google it and find the song and lyrics. It expresses the salvation experience, and the steps needed to become a born-again believer. The Christian faith is full of songs. They are written and sung by people who have experienced the birthing of their spirits. These songs are in response to God rescuing them. All songs are from the heart, and when we listen, we can decide to agree with them or not. Many a song, I will examine closely for the meanings. I like to sing with the radio. I also enjoy hearing good bible teachers. I immerse myself in the word and songs of love to God. My life is full of his joy.

Many songs talk about dying too. They speak of how death will be like crossing the Jordan River. It is a simile, and is not biblical. Death has been overcome by Jesus. He decides who and when. He also decides where we go when we die. I have a hope inside that I am a spirit living in a fleshly body. When this body wears out or is stricken with disease, I will have to relinquish this body and go to live with God in his Heaven. This body will be discarded, but I will live on. The flesh will be gone, but the soul and the spirit will live on. This is a great promise that Jesus gave to us. To be absent from the body is to be present with the Lord according to scripture.

Exchanges for my Sins

In exchange for my sins Jesus gave me a new life. I gave up several behaviors and Jesus redeemed them and gave them back to me to be properly enjoyed. You will remember my love for dancing had led me astray and had encouraged me to act sexually and provocative toward the opposite sex. God revealed that I was causing the man to lust physically with my gyrations. I was not supposed to cause another to sin. So even though I had the freedom to dance, I was to control my body so as not to arouse the man sexually, which could lead to his falling into sins. I was not to dress alluringly which could also cause the man to lust in his mind. I learned I was to dress and conduct myself the way that God wanted me to behave.

Causing another to sin is a terrible no no. Jesus said whoa to anyone who causes a little one to sin. It is better for him to have a millstone tied around his neck than to do this. A little one can have two meanings. It could mean a child underage of adulthood or a newborn believer is also referred to as a child. Jesus takes it very serious how our behaviors and freedoms affect others.

Later in life he gave me back my dancing. In my thirties I was introduced to square dancing. It was clean and wholesome. I enjoyed years of dresses and dances with much joy and peace. Then, later again, God gave me Contra dancing. This type of dancing was like barn dancing and provided me with much physical activity and social enjoyment. Both of these dancing styles were a blessing from God.

Another redemption that Jesus gave me was the alcohol exchange. As I explained earlier in the book the wine from Jesus is a strong wine that will get you drunk on his Spirit. So, I gave up natural wine for a more wonderful spiritual wine. God's wine did not leave you with a hangover either. I can drink till my heart's content.

When I was around four years old, I had stuck a knife in my eye and remained blind the rest of my life. The eye was deteriorating and causing people to look away from me when I spoke. In my fifties I received my miracle. I found an eye shield. It is a fake eye that you wear on top of your real eye. It had a painting of an eyeball that matched my other eye perfectly. It was wonderful. Jesus had given me back my appearance. It was like a new life. People no longer could tell the difference. My eye looked normal. Although the blindness remained, the disgrace and hiding of the deformation was gone. This transformation helped to build and restore my self-esteem.

Calling on the Power of God

Only a child of God has the right and power to call upon the name of God. When this occurs, all the world has to stop, obey and take notice that God's child is exercising his right and authority he received at his spiritual birth. When a child learns to pray and knows that his Father is listening, he is asking without doubts or disbelief. If he knows he will receive what he is praying for, then that believer is walking in obedience to the scriptures. He is in complete submission to God. This is the fervent prayer of the righteous believer, and it says they will receive much. They are practicing holiness, no deceit or guile will be uttered from their mouths, they will seek a life of purity. Their will is in agreement with God's will and their obedience allows the power of God to operate in their situations.

Steps I have Climbed

Letting the word of God transform me by reading to learn the plan of God has been my goal since the beginning of my walk with Jesus. Getting to know him by fellowshipping with him has helped me to attain knowledge of God and his Son's purpose for my life. This knowledge has incorporated the wisdom of God. I have seen my life manifest God's life as I have surrendered to his calling. Figuring out the plan of God and the various parts that had to be executed along the way. This is the greatest spiritual quest I could pursue. Learning about the two different covenants that are operating in the world today, that are still in effect, brings great assurance to my life. Exploring the authority of God and how Jesus operated in it.... Past, present, and future gives me strength and power.

Quick Overview

Deciphering God's messages to his people has been the challenge from day one. I have learned all about the creation and the beginning of human beings. You see I just cannot stick my head in the sand and refuse to view the fossil record. As I studied the origin of mankind, I realized that there were possibly pre-human beings who lived upon this planet. Now this population is not mentioned in the Bible because God is only concerned with his new creation Adam and Eve and their ancestry line. Some anthropologists agree that around 4000 BC man changed and homo sapiens began to inhabit the earth. The bible tells me that Jesus was the first born of the new creation and that we become a new creation when we receive the Holy Spirit inside of us. Adam and Eve were also a new creation.

That being said, we continue our quest for understanding. Now God told Adam and his heirs to not mix with the people of the other nations. He wanted to keep the blood line pure. It is my belief that when Noah, who was a righteous man, and his wife and sons all came off the ark there was still a trace of the stone age human in possibly one of the son's wives.

God cursed one of the grandchildren of Noah. That child, Canan, son of Ham, grows up to become a nation that later on God will have his children to deal with. Now we learn that at the time of creation, Satan is already occupying the world. God owns the creation that he calls the earth, but the world systems operating on God's earth is ruled by Satan.

God had created the earth and given the power and authority to Adam. Adam was tricked by Satan and lost that dominion. Now Satan owned Adam and his earthly kingdom. Adam became a slave to sin, and his master of sin was Satan.

God wanted to rescue his creation and help them to walk in freedom. So, he made covenants which are like treaties. He said if these people would let him be their God and worship and obey Him, then He would be their God constantly watching over them, protecting them from the enemies, and providing for them to meet their needs.

These descendants of Noah and their family tree can be traced in the book of Genesis. I love how God is so accurate, and it is amazing how he will lay out his entire plan to mankind if they will just take the time to read it for themselves.

The reader will learn about the great men of faith who believed God and his words, and how that faith in God was counted to them as righteousness. Even back in the beginning of time, God was extending his righteousness to his chosen people. Now as time passed, these children had more children and more children were born. Soon these people grew into a large population, and they were able to inhabit the land that was occupied by the other nations that did not have a covenant with God.

So finally, about 2,000 years have passed, and it is time to give God's people the land that He has promised. He picks Moses for this task. This is still all in the book of Genesis.

So, we begin the second book in the Bible called Exodus where the book of Genesis has ended. God delivers his people who have been taken captive as slaves in the land of Egypt. They come out with God's power and blessings. They now must follow Moses and learn how to hear God's voice and obey God's commands. It is in this book, The Ten Commandments are given and explained. We also learn that the law is a spiritual law and that the angels enforce adherence. They, the spiritual messengers for God, will accuse us of lawbreaking, or they will also report our obedience.

Now God did not give the law to put us in bondage. He said He was Holy and that He wanted to be with His people. But He could not allow them to come near Him if they were contaminated. His holiness would be a consuming fire, and they would suffer if they entered His presence without the covering. So, God developed the sacrificial system to help cleanse the people so they would receive His righteousness and favor. The blood sacrifice would fulfill the requirements. The reader then learns how important the Tabernacle and the elements were.

Throughout the reading God is demonstrating how much he cares about His people. He carefully deals with them about every kind of issue that could occur. He sets up a government system for them to follow. He wants to be their God. But people have a fallen nature, and they want someone to be in charge of them who they can see physically.

So, God gave them the Prophets to rule over them as they gradually acquired the new territories. As they took over parts of the land, they saw that these people had a king to rule them. Well, God said no, you do not need a king. He warned that a king will take advantage of your freedoms and make you servants. The people rebelled and demanded a king. So, the next few books are all about all the different kings that ruled the people during the different times of the eras. That will cover Kings and Chronicles.

Now the hardest part of the Old Testament is making sense about what is going on and the timeline taking place. God warns for decades that idolatry and worshipping the gods of the land will get them in trouble. Naturally, the people do not listen, and they then must suffer the consequences. There are several different times that different enemies attack them. Each one is to wake them up so they will remember what God has said. But the people disobey and rebel. The enemy comes. First it is the Assyrians who swoop down and take all ten northern tribes into captivity. It took me years to realize that these ten tribes never returned. They were swallowed up and assimilated into that empire. Then about another 100 years later, another nation called Babylon, who had previously conquered the Assyrian tribe, now comes against the last two southern tribes where Jerusalem is located. God had warned through the Prophets which is found in all the books in the back of the Old Testament. Now the nation of Israel had split during the reign of King Solomon. He was the son of King David. Anyway, the ten tribes were called Israel and the other two were called Judah. So, you have to keep that clear as you read. God says these two tribes are like sisters. He warns through the prophets that Judah could suffer the same exile if they do not stop all of their idolatry. They too are rebellious and suffer the same fate. There are some horrible descriptions of the siege they endure before being forced into slavery. But this time God had said only 70 years will be their punishment. So, He lets them return. These events are recorded in the books of Ezra and Nehemiah. They return to their homeland. They attempt to rebuild the temple.

Then The Old Testament goes quiet for about 400 years.

As a historian, I wanted to know what happened during these years. This was the arising of the Persian and Greek Empire. During the book of Daniel, we do learn that the Persians sneak into Babylon and conquer the nation. From now on they will constantly fight with their neighbors the Greeks. Finally, the Greeks will win their territory. During their glory they have the leader Alexander the Great. He is killed, and his territory is divided among his four generals.

Then after the Greeks the Roman Empire will emerge and they will have the rulers called Caesars. It is this government that will be in effect at the time of Jesus. When the New Testament begins, Jesus is arriving on the earth.

Why the Bible

I know this is just a quick overview of the first 4,000 years of the new creation. There is so much in the Bible that the believer needs to know and understand. I urge you to embrace this book and discover more about the God you serve.

Studying His words, His messages, His plans, were my pursuit, and then allowing God to reveal them to me. Discovering his purpose and execution of his perfect plan of redemption has been a lifetime pursuit. I was taught how to understand his death and his triumph over death and the grave. I spent years searching for truths continually asking questions. The truths and the answers are found in the word of God and in the hymns that speak the solid truths of Christianity.

Like any subject that we study, we must first learn the meanings of the words. That is called vocabulary. We want to be able to apply them to our spiritual walk. We hear these words whispered to our inner being while reading his words. Questioning what they mean and how do they apply in the spiritual believer's life, we seek to find the answers by putting it all together to form the bigger before and after picture.

The salvation message and all the parts that come with it are needed to be in play to recreate a human being into a Chistian. Jesus does it in a flash of a moment when the human believes his message. His transformation was planned and executed years ago. It is the believer's quest to respond to this wonderful free gift of salvation. It is his spiritual responsibility to pursue the pursuer who has revealed himself to them. He tells us do not neglect so great a salvation.

In the gospels we read of the ten lepers who were cleansed of leprosy. If this sickness is a symbolism for sin, it represents humanity. They were all healed. They all knew who had accomplished this act of salvation. But only one went and thanked Jesus for their miracle. One out of ten responded to Jesus. I find that quite interesting. Out of ten people who ask Jesus to forgive their sins, and he does that immediately, only one will give their life and follow him forever. I am still contemplating on this possibility.

I was held in captivity to the ruler of this world, Satan, prisoner to sin and death was my sentence. I was taken into the wilderness to learn to rely on God and his deliverance from the world. God was destroying the power of the world and its hold upon me. The freedom I received when I made Jesus my Lord was miraculous. I was extremely thankful for the deliverance I experienced.

When we, believers, first become a Christian, we are not very well seasoned in the word of God. We speak a broken scripture in phrases because we have not come to the full understanding of the complete scripture. So as babes in Christ, we are limited in different words we can use to witness with. Unfortunately, we can sound like a bumper sticker because it is hard to quote full scriptures. We only know a few short choppy phrases. We are very ignorant of the life that is waiting for us as we unwrap our present from Jesus and begin to read his words from his book, the Bible. It is this unknowing that inhibits us from witnessing to others. We are limited in our understanding and therefore we do not feel able to speak about our faith. But we have our testimony. It is perfectly ok to say we do not know that yet.

Conclusion

These are the spiritual truths I have learned in my many years of salvation. I am sure I have not begun to cover all the truths from the Bible.

These are the major lessons I was learning. I am now forty years old in the Lord.

I stop here because my life got a lot more messy before it was finally delivered to a peace in the Kingdom of God. Serving God has been extremely fulfilling and exciting. I have seen him work in my life and others in the most miraculous ways. I implore all who read this booklet to begin or continue to walk with Jesus. Do not let anything stand in your way of achieving a rich, faithful life in Him.

Your life will have meaning and purpose. You will experience all events with your spiritual eyes wide open and you will be able to cope and achieve many pursuits of your heart with Jesus in your heart. Normal events will have significance in a much deeper way. Life is best with Jesus inside and reigning on our thrones.

So, I have answered the call of God to record his mercy and favor that has been extended toward me in life. He did not demand that I write this story. He asked if I would like to write about Him and give Him the glory for all He has done for me and others in my life.

If while reading any part of this book, you felt the spirit was tugging on your heart, then you need to pray. Prayer is just talking to God. It does not have to be elegant. It needs to be you coming clean with God, and you asking him to help you understand his truths. You should acknowledge to him what you truly believe about him and his message. It is ok to tell him you do not believe. Tell him what is hanging you up. Ask him to reveal to you his presence. Be honest with Him and yourself. God already knows you, so do not try to pull the wool over his eyes. That would be unproductive.

I can say that I love the Lord with all my heart, mind, strength, and might. Now the next hurdle to face is how to get this story printed and in the hands of friends, family, acquaintances, and others.

I do not take pride and think that this booklet will become a best seller. I am not a great theological scholar who can speak elegantly. In fact, I plan on giving away these copies to those who would like one. It will be self-published because I do not want to charge people for my simple words of inspiration. They are for everyone who has the ability to hear in the spirit, and those who are still seeking. I pray that they have a grand effect upon the readers, and they will share their booklet with others along the way.

I am thanking you in advance for your assistance in spreading the words of life. If you desire to get in touch with me, I can be reached at my email. Nray@bledsoe.net , Or you can write to me at Nancy Ray 627 Lucille Dr. Lexington KY 40511.

* 9 7 9 8 3 3 0 3 9 5 7 0 5 *